# Copyright

# Contents

# Introduction

*STOP!* Before you turn to the first chapter, I think I should warn you – this book may not be for you!

If you love the idea of *Get Rich Quick, Retiring in Less Than a Year*, or if you're just dying to learn *How To Make A Fortune Getting a Network of People to Do All The Work For You* – sorry, you've got the wrong book.

What Jeffrey Babener and David Stewart have written in *The Network Marketer's Guide to Success* is a thorough, practical exploration of what you *really* need to know – and do – to start and build your own successful Network Organization. It's a solid, straightforward "Guide To Success" that takes you – one step at a time – through a proven process of creating your own prosperous, enduring Network Marketing business. If you take to heart and mind what you read here – that is, if you allow this book to *be your guide* – you *will* be successful in Network Marketing. It is the most comprehensive and accessible book on the subject I have read to date.

Jeffrey Babener is the world's leading legal counsel in the Network Marketing industry. He and his firm, Babener and Orcutt, are called upon routinely by corporations, distributor organizations and state and federal agencies as experts in Network Marketing Law. Throughout *The Network Marketer's Guide to Success*, you will share the benefits of Jeff Babener's years of research and experience. In one sense, this book is like having Jeffrey on retainer. What you will learn about the law, the various state and federal regulations, business planning and the substantial tax benefits you can realize from owning and operating your own Network Marketing enterprise, will serve your success for years to come. The advice you get in this book will guide you to increased earnings and savings worth many thousands of dollars.

David Stewart is a consummate Network Marketing professional. He's been in this business for over 20 years, during which time he has worked successfully with hundreds of Network Marketing companies and distributor organizations as a consultant and trainer. One of the things I enjoy most about David is how he stands with one foot firmly in Networking and the other planted solidly in Marketing. Too many times in our business, so-called trainers are either/or. David marries the two disciplines to create a nuts-an'-bolts approach to teaching people how to achieve Network Marketing success *that really works*. When he shows you the steps to take to reach a six-figure income – read and remember well. He has done it himself! – and he has taught many others – people just like you – to do it, too.

When we first began publishing the MLM *Success*™ newsletter, we saw a tremendous need in our industry for a compelling presentation-prospecting tool that would explain Network Marketing to people – once and for all, *clearly* and *powerfully*. We planned to write "the definitive brochure" that would appeal to the more professional people who are becoming interested in our business, establish real credibility in the prospect's mind and show how Network Marketing was a remarkable business opportunity and a solid, powerful investment for their future. A subscriber sent us a copy of Babener and Stewart's *Network Marketing – One*

*Plus One Equals Four*.  We aren't planning to write our brochure anymore.  They did it first and they did a great job. Our next project was to be a book on "How to Create Real Success in Network Marketing."  Now we aren't going to do that project, either! Jeffrey Babener and David Stewart have done that for us as well.

*The Network Marketer's Guide to Success* is a wonderful book.  I highly recommend reading it, using it, referring to it and sharing it with everyone in your Network Marketing Organization.

> John Milton Fogg
> Editor, MLM *Success*™
> Charlottesville, Virginia

## *Chapter 1*
# The Big Picture

*Network Marketing could be the
perfect vehicle for you to travel the
highway to success.*

# The Big Picture

An "Entrepreneurial Revolution" is sweeping the United States and Canada! It shouldn't surprise you. A dramatic shift in economic opportunity is predictable as a democratic society such as ours matures. The desire to become an entrepreneur, shared by an ever increasing number of men and women today, has grown from a wistful dream into a cultural revolution.

New alternatives to conventional retailing are rapidly changing the way North Americans buy and sell everything. Twenty years ago, franchising was a relatively new and misunderstood phenomenon. Today, more than $600 billion in annual sales is generated through franchises in the United States alone! Also 20 years ago, William Gates of Microsoft Software and Steven Jobs of Apple Computer were teenagers tinkering with new technologies in their garages. These young entrepreneurs created the global personal computer revolution. Today, they are two of the wealthiest men in the world.

The vast majority of new jobs created in the United States comes from small businesses with fewer than 20 employees. Small businesses are everywhere – in the city, in the suburbs and out in the country as well. In 1988, there were an estimated 14.9 million home-based businesses in America. The projection for 1989 was 18.3 million – a 23 percent increase in only one year! According to Rowan Wakefield, author of *Starting and Operating a Home-Based Business*, this figure should top 40 million by the year 2000. These entrepreneurial enterprises are laying the foundation for the future of our national economy! Remember, these are small, personal businesses–and their watchwords for success include: *personal service, convenience, quality and making a contribution to others.*

It is within this exciting arena of free enterprise that you'll find one of the fastest growing, most dynamic new ways of doing business in the world today – a unique and powerful approach to marketing and sales that is attracting the interest of the business community and general public alike – Network Marketing. Network Marketing includes both Multi-Level Marketing (MLM) and Direct Selling.

It is rapidly catching the interest – *and spending dollars* – of giant corporations, consumers and entrepreneurs all over the world. Here's why.

**For Corporations**, Network Marketing represents an extraordinary marketing opportunity. For a producer with the right goods or services, the Network Marketing method of distribution and sales can significantly reduce the "conventional" costs of doing business – such as advertising, merchandising and selling expenses – while dramatically increasing overall sales. That claim alone is enough to get their attention in a very big way.

**For Consumers,** Network Marketing offers unique and often superior products and services not available through normal retail channels, such as stores and mail order – *plus* the welcome convenience of time-saving, at-home shopping. In addition, Network Marketing *directly rewards consumers* both for their *loyalty* – with discounts for continued purchases – and for their *advocacy* – by actually paying people for recommending the products to others.

**For Entrepreneurs**, Network Marketing presents the *lowest cost* business start-up possible. Couple this with the benefits of working for yourself, part-time or full-time as you choose, from your home, realizing thousands of dollars in immediate tax savings, and the personal and professional freedom of a Network Marketing lifestyle, *plus* its powerful, proven, six-figure earning potential – and you just may have the perfect business opportunity!

Today, Network Marketing in the U.S. and Canada (and in the world) is very big business. Industry experts estimate that in 1989 it was a $20 billion industry growing at 30 percent annually. Approximately one in 10 households in the United States has someone involved in Network Marketing. Estimates are that 90 percent of the 12 million Network Marketers (1989 figures) are part-time, but an increasing number of men and women are choosing to make it a full-time career. Statistical surveys indicate that 60 to 70 percent of North American households have purchased goods and services from Network Marketers.

## Network Marketing Companies

The corporate players of Network Marketing are by no means "lightweights." They are Fortune 500 and New York Stock Exchange (NYSE) companies. The largest cosmetics company in the world, Avon, with sales in excess of $3 billion, is a Direct Selling company. The A. L. Williams Corporation, the largest seller of individual life insurance every year since 1984 (placing more coverage of this type than Prudential), is a Network Marketing company. The Amway Corporation of Ada, Michigan, with U.S. sales approaching $2 billion and more than one million distributors, has *exported* its success, too. Amway Japan, with annual Japanese sales in excess of $600 million, is one of the 10 fastest growing foreign corporations. That ranks Amway (whose name was coined as an abbreviation of "the American Way") with the likes of IBM and Mobil Oil!

Colgate-Palmolive markets through its Network subsidiary, Princess House; so does the Gillette Company, through its subsidiary, Jafra Cosmetics. Shaklee Corporation has grown to be a diversified New York Stock Exchange company once coveted by Wall Street raiders and ultimately acquired by a large Japanese conglomerate. Mary Kay Cosmetics is both a household word and a recent NYSE company, now taken private. U.S. Sprint and MCI have garnered in excess of three million customers on the playing fields of Network Marketing. Network Marketing companies have gained renown and respect both as new product pioneers in North American markets and for revitalizing the sales of products which had languished for years on the retail shelf. The Network Marketing industry literally created a multi-million dollar market for home water-filtration systems, and now accounts for the sale of more than 50 percent of all the water filters sold in the United States.

One of the most celebrated success stories in recent years has been the extraordinary accomplishments of Lane Nemeth and her company, Discovery Toys. Ms. Nemeth noticed the delight and enthusiasm of parents and teachers for the superior quality educational toys she brought from Europe. Signing on teachers and parents as distributors, Nemeth revealed an entirely new demographic market for the products. Her business has experienced astonishing success, with sales approaching $75 million.

## Successful Network Marketers

While Network Marketing companies obviously have prospered, corporate success is less than half the story. Individual men and women from all walks of life have found remarkable success and financial security by building their own organizations of Networking distributors. Where else could a 22-year-old hotel bellman begin his own small business, with less than $500 capital investment, and three years later be enjoying a monthly income of $35,000? Or how about a retired engineer and his wife who now earn more than $25,000 a month? A young former business executive, after only two years in the business, is receiving royalty overrides that equal a $250,000 annual income. A husband and wife team, 20-year veterans of the Networking industry, earn *one million dollars a year* through their growing distributorship!

Perhaps most impressive is the lady in her 40s who runs her Network Marketing business part-time out of her home – *while bringing up four teenagers* – and has managed to build a $20,000 monthly income within two short years! These are only a few of the thousands of people who have found tremendous personal satisfaction and richly rewarding financial success through Network Marketing.

## The Future of Network Marketing

The indicators show clearly that the trend of explosive growth for Network Marketing will continue far into the future. Corporate America will increasingly rely on Network Marketing as an alternative method of distribution for a variety of fundamental reasons:

1)   Network Marketing is a perfect, low cost, minimal risk way to introduce new and unrecognized products into the marketplace.

2)   This method of distribution and sales may even be *a necessity* for information rich, value added products or services with a "high education" factor that require personal demonstration and explanation.

3)   Network Marketing is a superb method for motivating and rewarding "consumer advocacy" – the natural human tendency to share our excitement and enthusiasm about a product by recommending it to our family and friends.

4)   Network Marketing can achieve rapid and thorough penetration of specifically targeted segments of the marketplace more easily than any other method.

5)   Network Marketing is efficient and economical com-

pared to the tremendous advertising, merchandising and promotional costs and escalating "cost of sales" for the conventional introduction of new products or services into the marketplace.

The business sections of bookstores throughout America are bursting with new  releases about how to become an entrepreneur and start your own small business. *The New York Times'* "bestseller list" *always* includes a number of titles on business, management and successful selling. Magazines such as *Entrepreneur, Venture, Inc.* and even *Forbes* have become important – *and well read* – fixtures in U.S. and Canadian homes. Audio cassettes dealing with issues involved in managing a business, starting a business, sales, motivation, marketing and general "business wisdom" are impossible for stores to keep in stock. Many North Americans now read the business section of daily newspapers *before* turning to the sports page and comics! Yes, our society is in the process of rapid and sweeping change. In fact, it is in the midst of a cultural revolution!

## The New Marketing

The primary growth in distribution and sales throughout the economy in recent years has come mainly from alternative marketing. As we said, franchise sales now account for *more than one-third* of all U.S. retail sales! Publication of direct mail catalogs has exploded in recent years, resulting in annual sales volume in excess of $100 billion! Home shopping cable TV channels have accounted for unexpected, explosive sales growth in just a few short years. Telemarketing represents a major new industry – an awesome selling power-house – in the United States. We are on the eve of the blast-off of shopping and banking via home-computers. Clearly, North Americans more than appreciate these new alternative methods for purchasing products and services –

*they are demanding them*!

Recent demographic studies indicate that during the next 10 years, 50 percent of existing middle-level management employees will be looking for new jobs. As the baby boom generation reaches mid-level management age, its 76 million members will all be competing for the same jobs. At the same time, U.S. and Canadian corporations, in their efforts to cut costs and streamline operations, are shrinking the available job market for those positions! The result? – over the next several years, we will see a huge army of educated, experienced, mature baby boomers *with the added responsibilities of caring for a family* forced to look for new ways to earn a living. Where will they turn? One place is for sure – Network Marketing.

In 1979, the Federal Trade Commission, in a landmark decision involving Amway, recognized the legitimate status of Network Marketing as a business opportunity. Congressional legislation and the Tax Equity Fairness Responsibility Act (TEFRA), in 1982, specifically recognized the "independent contractor status" of Direct Sellers. The IRS publishes its own booklets specifically for Network Marketers. Many states have adopted legislation recognizing the legitimacy of Network Marketing and offer a system of guidance similar to that designed earlier for educating the franchise industry. In recent years, business schools and major universities throughout the United States have adopted curricula and conducted case studies dealing with Network Marketing companies. Network Marketing enterprises are regularly featured in national magazines. And the industry now has two active, national trade associations.

In short, Network Marketing's place in "the mainstream" is assured.

## Why Network Marketing?

For individuals interested in being part of the Entrepreneurial Revolution, Network Marketing offers exceptional possibilities.

1. Where else can you *start your own business*, working for yourself, *with such minimal cost or capital investment* – often as little as a few hundred dollars?

2. Network Marketing offers you *the choice of a part-time business or full-time career* involvement. That gives anyone employed in a regular job the ability to earn much needed extra income, and it allows the beginning entrepreneur the rare ability to "earn while you learn."

3. What other professional occupation offers the very real potential of earning $500 to $1000 per month part time, and $5000, $10,000, or more a month full time – *without years of experience or college and post graduate education?*

4. In an increasingly isolated and unfriendly world, Network Marketing offers you tremendous opportunity for expanding your social environment by meeting and working together with new friends who share common values and ideals. In Network Marketing, you'll never have to "do it by yourself."

5. Network Marketing offers you very real, *immediate tax benefits* because of the *self-employed status* and the advantages of *a home-based business*. Many business commentators now argue that Network Marketing is one of the last true bastions of tax relief.

6. Most products offered via Network Marketing are extremely high quality, often one-of-a-kind, information rich goods and services which consumers will not commonly find in conventional retail stores, in mail order catalogs or by other means.

7. Finally, and perhaps most importantly, men and women in Network Marketing *take responsibility for their own lives* and are richly rewarded for their unique talents and abilities. Above all, Network Marketing *is a lifestyle* – a lifestyle of self-esteem, of making a difference and of personal and professional freedom.

## What Is Network Marketing?

Network Marketing is a remarkable opportunity for you to create a business enterprise of your own – and much more. It is a revolutionary approach to distribution and sales that uniquely combines two powerful ideas in a new and different way – *Networking* and *Marketing*.

*Marketing* is the movement of goods and services through the distribution channel, from manufacturer to end consumer. This includes the consumer's continuing satisfaction with the benefits of those goods and services over time. *Networking* is the coming together of numbers of people who share information and resources working together to accomplish their common goals.

In some ways, a Network Marketing enterprise operates in the same way as any conventional company engaged in distribution and sales.

In Network Marketing, for instance, you develop a network of distributors through which a company's products or services are exchanged directly with the ultimate consumer. Your profits are derived from commissions on your personal sales, as well as bonus, or "override" commissions earned from the total sales volume of all the other distributors in your personal network or downline sales organization.

Profits are earned by distributors who buy products from the Network Marketing company at wholesale and sell them at retail. In other cases, a distributor may simply take orders and receive commissions from the sales of those products or services. This is actually the same method of compensation paid by conventional marketing companies to their commissioned sales representatives. One key difference is that in a conventional company, *you are their employee.* In Network Marketing, you are their *partner. You are an independent contractor working in your own business – and you are your own boss.*

Conventional companies also have substantial advertising and marketing budgets they use to generate sales. Out of this budget they compensate sales managers for the recruitment, training, and management of their sales organization and its individual sales representatives. Sales Managers in these companies generally are responsible for the sales activity of a number of sales people assigned to specific territories. In a Network Marketing company, the independent contractor is responsible for assembling his or her own network of distributors, and for training and managing them as well. Also, Network Marketing rarely involves specified sales territories. Within the marketing rights of the company involved, Network Marketers are free to build national (and even international) organizations of their own.

Conventional companies spend a great deal of money on advertising and sales promotion (merchandising, trade shows, in-store sampling and demonstrations, discounting, etc.) in the hopes of stimulating initial interest to try their products and maintaining a growing demand for their products over time. Here too, Network Marketing departs *dramatically* from the way conventional companies operate.

## Every Marketer's Goal

Traditional marketers use a three step process in the attempt to accomplish sales of their products and services.

**1.** *Trial.* This is where potential customers are persuaded to try the "unknown" product for the first time.

**2.** *Consumer Franchise.* This is a customer who has tried the product, likes it, and continues to purchase that specific product brand again and again.

**3.** *Consumer Advocacy.* This is a satisfied customer who recommends that specific brand of product or service to others.

Obviously, people must try a new product. If they don't, there will be no sales and no company.   Getting people to make that first purchase (Trial) is an expensive task. Major marketers spend millions of dollars to stimulate people's interest and attention for their products, and then even more is spent to bring them into the stores to make that initial purchase. Establishing a loyal customer base (Consumer Franchise) also is a must for any marketer. And the best of all marketing worlds is one filled with people who recommend your product (Consumer Advocates) through that most compelling and powerful form of advertising – *word of mouth.*

## Enthusiasm Is the Key to Success

It's natural to be excited and enthusiastic about a great product or service. When you discover a terrific restaurant, read a fascinating book or are turned on to something that really makes a difference in how you look and feel – what do you do? You share your enthusiasm for that "product" with your family and friends. The extraordinary beauty and power of Network Marketing is that the Network Marketing company *rewards you directly* for recommending its products or services. And the more you recommend them, the greater your rewards. Would your life be any different if you'd been given, say, $5.00, every time a friend of yours bought a product just because you encouraged them to do so? You bet. That's Network Marketing.

Instead of having a huge advertising and marketing budget, Network Marketing companies take that money and compensate *you* – the distributor – for creating the product *trial*, for establishing a *consumer franchise*, and for your own and others' *consumer advocacy* for the company's products or services.

Now, in truth, any good salesman or saleswoman is a "consumer advocate." A sales person who loves his or her product is quite irresistible. The difference in Network Marketing is *who* does that job – and *how many* of those *whos* it takes to do it.

## Lots of People, Each Doing a Little

Conventional sales is a few people each doing a whole lot of work. A company-employed, commissioned salesperson must move a tremendous volume of products in order to earn a decent living. In Network Marketing, it's just the opposite. By building a growing Network of men and women who love the products and simply recommend them to the family members and friends in their immediate "circle of influence" – you get a lot of people each doing a little. If you were successfully to recommend a product to just one person a month, starting today, and each of those people did the same thing – successfully recommended the product to just one person each month – how many people would be using the product in one year? 4,096!

What would that mean in dollars? Let's assume a realistic average product purchase of $50 per month from each person in the Network, and let's say each person successfully recommended the same amount of product to just one other person – a retail customer who wasn't in the Network; finally, we'll also assume you'd earn a conservative 10% commission on your Network Organization's total sales volume. In one year, your business would be earning $80,000 annually. Network Marketing is a lot of people, each doing just a little – and adding up to a whole lot!

## The Networker's Rewards

In Network Marketing, the individual distributor receives a bonus override on sales of sponsored distributors – in part, as compensation for training, managing and encouraging sales and recruitment. These distributors, in turn, do the same thing. You earn a bonus override on the product sales made by those distributors you have sponsored, as well as on the sale of products by those they sponsor, by those *they* sponsor, and so on. These bonuses are earned on several levels of distributors in your Network Organization. The number of levels and the percentage or dollar value of the commissions and bonuses all depend on your particular company's compensation structure. In other words, distributors receive both commissions for the direct sale of products they move personally and an override type of bonus for the sales made by the distributors they have sponsored and trained, those *they* have sponsored and trained, and so on.

When you become a distributor, you work independently and develop your own Network Organization – but the Network Marketing company also serves as your "partner in profit." The company researches, develops and packages the product, handles all the data processing and shipping for you, and creates the sales aids and training programs you use to support your distributors. This valuable assistance enables and empowers distributors to determine their own course – to determine how quickly they want to become financially successful and how they want to build their own businesses – and yet, because of the company's support and the awesome power of Networking – you *never have to do it alone.*

## You Are the Bottom Line

The uniqueness of Network Marketing is that YOU determine what the results and rewards will be. YOU create, direct and manage your own destiny. Your time and your life belong to YOU. In Network Marketing, perhaps for the first time in your life – certainly in your working life – YOU have the opportunity TO BE FREE!

# Chapter 2
# Network Marketing and the Law

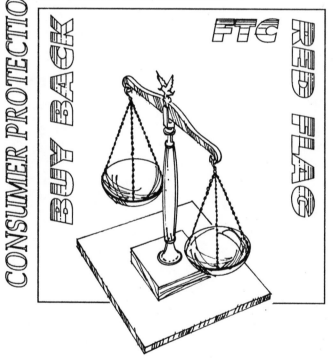

*... and nothing but the truth about what makes a legal, successful Networking Business.*

# Network Marketing and the Law

## First, Why Are We Telling You All This?

Network Marketing (including Direct Selling and Multi-Level Marketing) is unfortunately a misunderstood industry in the minds of much of the general public. Negative publicity and the misguided actions of some unscrupulous individuals are responsible for that attitude. Contrary to conventional wisdom, the public *does not* have a short memory. At some time in your career, you will have to deal with a person who holds a negative impression of our industry.

This is a vital concern when you make a presentation. All too often, a Network Marketing Distributor will deliver an enthusiastic, informative, even inspiring presentation to a prospect, only to get a totally unexpected "No thanks, I'm not interested" – *which had nothing to do with his or her product or opportunity*! That "No" came from an already existing defense against Network Marketing which the prospect had well established in his or her mind. It was there from the start, and the entire presentation never got through it. What a waste of time. It's far better to reveal this issue *right up front* and address it *right then and there*. We've found that the direct approach works best.

## Take a Positive Approach

You can extol the virtues of Network Marketing in the first part of your presentation or in your meeting. Don't spend much time on this, and don't be defensive. Use some of the industry growth figures we gave you in the first chapter – and cite some of the prominent names in the business. Avon, A.L. Williams and Mary Kay are very impressive companies with outstanding track records and fine public acceptance. Use them to help make the case for the industry's credibility. If your prospects ask, explain the difference between legitimate Network Marketing companies and illegal pyramid schemes. Simply explain that the difference is *The Product*. Network Marketing deals in legitimate products and services that provide real value and benefit to the consumer. Tell them that the way you earn money in Network Marketing is *only* on the sales made by you and the men and women in your Network. Of course, share your excitement and personal experience of Network Marketing – the people, the products and the company. That's the best.

## The Current Legal Climate

Network Marketing companies are, in general, operational in every state in the United States, throughout all provinces in Canada and in an increasing number of foreign countries, such as England, Australia and Japan. Although the industry is not without its challenges, our federal and state governments openly offer assistance to Network Marketing companies, much the way they did in the early days of the franchising industry. The IRS has released special educational publications and videos, and has adopted specific regulations recognizing Network Marketing as a legitimate profession. Several states also have adopted specific legislation for Network Marketing companies that establish objective guidelines and standards for those companies to follow.

Any industry that offers such remarkable benefits, such dramatic economic potential and such a low cost of entry will tend to attract every conceivable sort of entrepreneur. Network Marketing has more than its fair share of every kind – good *and* bad – and over the years it has had its share of difficulties as well. At times, our business has come perilously close to extinction as a result of "aggressive" prosecution by regulators who claimed the industry promoted pyramid schemes, chain letter type opportunities and illegal lotteries, all under the guise of legitimate marketing enterprises. In many cases, they were right. And thankfully, in many others – they were wrong.

In a classic legal decision in 1979, the Amway Corporation prevailed in just such a prosecution. In essence, Amway received a "stamp of approval" by the Federal Trade Commission (FTC). This decision was a landmark case that opened the door for many of today's most successful Network Marketing companies.

Because of the abuse that has occurred in the past, Network Marketing has become a highly regulated and closely scrutinized industry. What is most unfortunate is that the regulations vary considerably from state to state in the United States, and are at best an ever-changing patchwork of laws which lack uniformity. Even within a given state government, one body often interprets the regulations differently from another. There are, however, some central themes that are treated similarly by all states.

## Consumer Protection Is the Key

The basic thrust of these statutes is to protect consumers from fraud, such as marketing plans that *require investment or purchase by a sales representative for the right to recruit others for his or her own economic gain*. Simply stated, this is the biggest "Red Flag" of all. When no real exchange of value takes place in a financial transaction – other than the ability to allow new people to "play the game" – that's a chain letter or illegal pyramid scheme. The now infamous "Airplane Game" is a classic example.

A player in the Airplane Game paid from hundreds to thousands of dollars for a "seat" on the "plane." Then, by virtue of enrolling a certain number of new "passengers," he or she moved up the rows of "seats" eventually to become a "co-pilot" and finally a "pilot." All of the money collected by the existing passengers to fill the vacant seats was given to the person who had advanced to pilot. Hundreds of people across the country became pilots and made tens of thousands of dollars. Tens of thousands *more* people *lost* from $1500 and up – often *way* up – when the airplane crashed, due to the inability to fill the seats or by intervention of local law enforcement officials shutting down the game. A number of players got the chance to fly straight to jail.

## What Makes a Legitimate Network Marketing Company

Network Marketing companies *must be* bona fide retail sales organizations which market legitimate products or services to the ultimate consumer. Recruiting, or "head hunting" for profit is strictly prohibited. So is inventory "front-loading." This is a process by which an unscrupulous company may try to require a substantial cash outlay for a large volume of product of questionable value from a new distributor. Often there is no real market for the distribution of the product other than the distributor's garage. This required "investment" is often in exchange for rapid advancement to the upper achievement levels of a marketing-compensation plan. Such practices not only come under the scrutiny of state regulators with Network Marketing concerns, they may also be looked at by federal agencies. Companies with "phony" product requirements are in reality scams masquerading as legitimate Network Marketing opportunities.

Also, a legitimate company does not charge a substantial fee from – nor make a profit on – a new distributor when he or she first "signs up." Sales kits and distributor manuals are sold at actual company cost to prevent this from occurring.

## The Key Legal Issues

Following is a list of the primary areas of concern for regulatory agencies. They are the "red flags" that attract the attention of these law enforcement officials to a potential abuse of the laws.

1. **Products that have "no real world" marketplace,** i.e., the marketing plan itself is the actual "product."

2. **Products that are sold at inflated prices.** If a similar item costs $25 in a conventional retail outlet, but the Network Marketing company is selling it for $100, that's a problem. Obviously, the "real" value here is in the compensation plan.

3. **Programs that require inventory loading.** Company programs should not require purchases of unreasonable amounts of inventory. Distributors should be told to buy for their reasonable foreseeable needs.  On the other hand, distributors cannot effectively sell without inventory on hand.

4. **"Uncalled for" substantial cash investment requirements.** Many states consider $500 or more to be "substantial." That's an investment governed by state's "business opportunity" laws as well.

5. **Mandatory purchase of peripheral or accessory products or services.** A great $50 product that can only be used with $2500 worth of additional fixtures is a scam.

6. **Programs that don't "buy back."** Any plan that does not

agree in writing to repurchase a reasonable percentage of unsold inventory or unused sales aids materials for a reasonable time after purchase from a terminating distributor.

7. **Fees paid for recruiting.** Any program that pays bonuses or commissions for the act of recruiting or "head hunting," rather than the sale of product.

8. **Earnings misrepresentations.** "Pie-in-the-sky" earnings claims and projections and "get rich quick" easy-money presentations are big problems!

In determining whether or not a given program is a legitimate Network Marketing opportunity, the following important points should be considered.

### Product or Service

The company should be offering a high quality product or service which is in demand in the marketplace. You may encounter a brand new product which, as yet, isn't in demand. However, once people learn of its benefits, you must be able to "make a market" based on demand for the product. The Sony "Walkman" is a perfect example. Consumer satisfaction should also be guaranteed. If the product is consumed by distributors themselves, it must be something they would buy based on its own merits exclusive of the money making opportunity.

### Price

The price of the product or service must be fair and it must be competitive in the marketplace. Distributors should be able to purchase the product at wholesale or at a reasonable discounted price relative to similar products found in retail stores.

### Investment Requirement

There should be *no* investment requirement at all other than a "sales kit." Sales kits should be purchased at company cost, as should any *required* demonstration material.

### Purchase and Inventory Requirements

There should be no minimum purchase requirement or inventory requirement in order to become a distributor. However, monthly qualifications are a reasonable facet of most Network Marketing compensation programs.

### Use of Product

Products should be used by the ultimate consumer. After all, this is the whole purpose of the marketing organization.

### Sales Commissions

Commissions should not be paid for recruiting or sponsoring. Nor should commissions be paid for sales aid materials.

### Buy Back Policy

A legitimate Network Marketing company will agree to re-purchase product inventory and sales materials in usable condition for some reasonable period of time from distributors who cancel their participation in the program.

### Retail Sales

The focus of the marketing program should be to promote product or service sales to consumers and non-participants in the program. Many states recognize that the wholesale purchase of company products in reasonable amounts for personal and family use is a tangible benefit of the program, and consider these to be legitimate "retail" sales.

### Distributor Activity

Many new statutes regarding Network Marketing companies require that distributors perform a bona fide supervisory or management role in terms of the sales and marketing function of moving company products through distribution to the end consumer. This would require some degree of consistent communication and contact from a sponsoring distributor to the members of his or her Network Organization.

## Earnings Representations

The basic rule here is that any earnings representation must be based on an actual track record. Recruiting advertisements should display fair and reasonable potential income based as well on actual fact. Explanations of earning possibilities listed in company manuals and brochures should be for instruction and educational purposes only – i.e., to explain the workings of the plan – and *are not* to be used as the basis for a distributor's specific earning expectations. Although the practice of a personal earnings testimonial by individual distributors is common, individuals should be careful not to get carried away. There is still no such thing as a "free lunch." Real and lasting income is simply the result of smart and hard work.

## Training

A good Network Marketing program should offer a solid training program for all its distributors. This is a key point. There may actually come a time when training becomes a *legally required* ingredient for a legitimate Network Marketing program. At present, it is "only" a fundamental business building tool, and not the law.

---

The future of the Network Marketing industry will require cooperation by all its member companies, industry trade associations, individual distributors and those state and federal agencies charged with its regulation and supervision. The greater the degree of "self-regulation" the industry can bring to bear on its own – the better. The single most valuable element in any successful enterprise is *integrity*. The key to Network Marketing and its good relationship with the Law – *is active and aware participation in the legal process by each and every one of us.*

# Chapter 3
# Your Ideal Business

YOU CAN HAVE IT ALL

*Who says you can't have it all?*
*Network Marketing says you can.*
*Here's how.*

# Your Ideal Business

**W**hy should you be so excited? Should you be congratulated?

Yes! Because you've made a decision to become a Network Marketer. It's a profound choice that will change your life forever. Congratulations!

The Network Marketing business you develop will be *your own*. Now you have the opportunity to create your personal and professional life *the way you've always thought it should be*. You're going to let the free market determine your value based on your own unique individuality – your creativity, talent and commitment. There's no more boss or impersonal system telling you how much he, she or it thinks you're worth. People and systems aren't always fair and objective in the way they evaluate their employees' performances.

So just how good is your opportunity in Network Marketing? Listed here are what a group of independent business experts, after much research and investigation, have determined are the components of the "Ideal Business." This research was not done for your specific company, nor even to establish standards for the Network Marketing industry in general. Its purpose is to help determine the odds of success for any business venture you might entertain. Let's see how your particular business opportunity in Network Marketing measures up.

### 1.   You Want a Business that Sells to the World.

You *never* want to be constrained in your marketing efforts. Do you have a universally accepted product line? One that is not limited to a single demographic group or geographic area? One that appeals to the broadest possible scope and greatest possible number of potential consumers? You should have the opportunity to market your product line openly throughout the country without restriction. You must be able to move your operation from Philadelphia to Arizona and still remain in the same business with access to a substantial consumer base. In other words, your business must be "flexible" and "portable."

### 2.   Your Products or Services Must Be in Demand.

What is the actual demand for your product or service? You must either provide a new and better way to meet your consumers' existing needs and wants, or offer them a new technology or new "best way of doing things" they've never seen before. The key word is *new*. You need to have a wide-open opportunity to meet or create a demand for your products or services. Otherwise, there would be no opportunity – and no business.

### 3.   The Demand Must Be Continuing.

Ideally, your product is consumable, which means there will be reorders from satisfied customers over time. Or, it should be a service for which there is a continuing need. If it is a durable product, your company must be committed to research and development of product improvements and the expansion of the product line with new items that fit the needs and wants of your existing market. In addition, what you offer should be something that consumers will continue to enjoy, from which they can learn or will continue to experience increasing benefits – *year after year*. Happy, satisfied customers beget more new customers, who beget

more new customers, and so on. You provide the supply –
continuing demand is what "grows" your business.

### 4. Low Overhead (This Is a Biggie).

Today, home-based businesses have become a very big
business, and this will be one of the major contributing
factors to your success. Having to pay the high overhead of
a separate office and all that entails dramatically decreases
the profitability of most types of businesses – especially at the
start. There is no need for an expensive facility nor for most
of the other operating expenses associated with being in
business – *if you're home-based*. You can start up and continue
profitably operating from your own home. Let the company
take the capital risks – not you.

And one more thing – *tax benefits*. As we mentioned in
Chapter 1, the home-based business aspect of your own
Network Marketing enterprise is one of the most tangible
forms of tax relief available. It immediately represents real
cash savings that easily can add thousands of dollars to your
income each year. We'll discuss this in detail in Chapter 14.

### 5. Special Products or Services.

The ideal business provides a product that is unique. It
should be difficult to copy or reproduce, i.e., "me-too" or
commodity products are *not* desirable. The only way they
become profitable is with an extremely high volume of sales
and the lowest possible price. And, like the "fastest gun in the
west," there is always another competitor with a cheaper
product at a "better" price. Quality is the key. Your product
*must* be a high quality item with exclusive, tangible and
recognizable benefits. And it should not be available in most
common retail outlets.

### 6. The "Ideal Business" Requires a Low Investment.

Just how much capital does it take to get started in
business? Normally, *far too much!*

For example, franchises are considered extremely attractive because of their relatively "low" cost of entry – anywhere from $25,000 to $500,000 or more! Obviously, they are not for the beginner. The average person doesn't (or shouldn't) start out in business with a franchise. Even starting a small local business without franchise fees can require every dollar the average person has saved and every dollar he or she can beg, borrow, or... and that's just for starters.

There is little (*if any*) guarantee or assurance of success in any new business venture. A common rule of thumb is that you should expect to go for at least one full year with no income at all! (And needless to say, the rate of small business failures during the first one to three years is alarmingly high.) So you're forced to start out deeply in debt – yet the whole idea of owning your own business was to create the financial success to get you out of debt *in the first place*!

How much capital would you need to make a decent return from any investment? What does it take in real estate, in stocks and bonds, or to generate enough interest earned from depositing long-term money in the bank? Any of these investments requires a *minimum* of *hundreds of thousands* of dollars simply to generate a few thousand dollars of earned income each month. No, investments are out of the question for any but the already-always rich.

However, Network Marketing is different. A distributor kit and a realistic sampling of product inventory usually is all that is required to get started. From $100 to $400 is a reasonable range to expect. Even with an investment in additional inventory for retail sales plus sales support and training materials, you're in business for a relatively small (in truth, *ridiculously small*) amount of money. You don't have to put yourself deeply in debt just to get started in Network Marketing. In fact, you can make a profit *your very first month* – *if* you follow the proven principles outlined in this book.

## 7. The "Ideal Business" Is a Cash Business.

You don't have to worry about credit terms or how to collect money from people who owe it to you – *if yours is a cash business*. When people owe you money, your business is financing their business. *Do not* go into the banking business unless that's what you intended to do! "A bird in the hand is worth two in the bush" – and if the bird is cash, it's worth a whole flock of uncollected receivables.

## 8. What About Regulations and the Law?

If you were considering going into business in any of the trades or as a professional – such as in medicine, law or accounting – there would be licensing fees and legal requirements. These requirements would cost you money, time and effort, and they require extensive education and expertise that you probably don't have and certainly do not want to deal with. While you don't have these requirements to hinder you in Network Marketing, there are industry guidelines as well as state and federal laws that must be followed by companies and independent distributors alike. There is no business that escapes state and local government regulation. Network Marketing is no exception. However, Network Marketing *does not* require you to be subjected to long, drawn out legal proceedings, high expenses or other complications. For the most part, your company has handled all of that for you. In fact, you can begin your Network Marketing *today* with a minimum of legal fuss.

------------

Now that you know the factors involved in an ideal business, ask yourself this question: "Does my Network Marketing opportunity meet these requirements – and how well does it fit?" We think you'll find it fits – "ideally."

If you see that this is true, go on to Chapter 4 – it will tell you how to get your "Ideal Business" started.

## Chapter 4
# Getting Started: Setting Up a Home-based Business

*The Network Marketing lifestyle is the best of both worlds: A successful professional working at home.*

# Getting Started: Setting Up a Home-based Office

Now we're going to share with you how to set up a complete, even ideal, home-based business office. You could approach this in a "seat-of-the-pants" fashion. However, by making the time *now* to do it right, you'll save yourself valuable future time *and* money. Depending upon your resources, you may have to follow this process in stages as you can afford it. The fact that you can earn money almost immediately in your Network Marketing business (remember, "earn while you learn") will be helpful in establishing a comfortable working environment as quickly as possible.

## Did You Make the Right Decision?

Before we start the list of what to do and what to get, let's talk just a bit about the very first problem facing every decision maker... *doubt*. The minute we make a choice, the very next thing that happens is to experience doubt as to whether or not that choice was correct. It's natural. The adage that applies here is, "Don't sweat the small stuff." And the real secret to success is – *it's all small stuff!*

Someone – usually a close friend or family member – is bound to tell you that, "Many people feel that there is something unprofessional about operating a home-based business." They may also encourage you to take steps to hide that fact from the business community. Thank them for their help, and – *don't believe it for a minute*! Economic forecasters predict that by the early 1990s, as much as 20 percent of the entire U.S. work force will be *exclusively home-based*. Remember, in Chapter One we told you there are currently 18.3 million businesses operating out of the home – a 23 percent increase in only one year! Not only is there absolutely nothing to be ashamed about if you conduct business from your home – in fact, you are a genuine pioneer riding the wave of the future. As long as your dealings are honest and you conduct yourself in a business-like manner, *you're home free*. And freedom is what this is all about.

## Smile When You Say "Uncle"

Many of the recommendations we'll be making in this chapter will enable your business relationships with the Internal Revenue Service to be much more "cordial." At one time (and to some extent, even today), a home-based business made IRS personnel sit up and take notice. In many cases, such a declaration meant an automatic audit. That IRS practice has diminished dramatically. Imagine, 18.3 million automatic audits – *no way*. It *does not mean*, however, that your business will not be subject to close scrutiny. It *does not mean* that you can avoid keeping good records. It *does mean* that as of this writing, home-based businesses may be one of the few kinds of tax-advantaged businesses around today. There is much more detailed information about your business – home and away – and the IRS in Chapter 14.

Here's our list of things to do. Remember, we're not suggesting you spend lots of money or remodel your home to accommodate your new office. Although, you *may* establish such a successful business so quickly that you require a new 1600 sq. ft. addition with beamed ceilings and skylights, four more phone lines, two computers, audio-video system, paging system, car phone, training facilities to accommodate, say, 50 or 60 Networkers, a pool... well, you'll see.

Seriously, here's your list:

1. **Plan carefully** when determining where your office should be located in your home. To satisfy IRS requirements, it should be an area – preferably a separate room or rooms – that you use *exclusively* for your business. If it is also used as a sewing room, a place for your children's model train layout, or a frequently used spare room, you cannot legitimately claim that entire portion of your home's square footage as business use for tax purposes.

If you have children or pets in your home, we recommend a room that can be isolated by a closed door (a secure door is a must, a lockable door may be even better). It will be frustrating to return to your office one day and find that your important business papers have been scribbled all over with red crayon by a budding artist or chewed by a teething puppy. If you invite customers or associates to your office, it's important that children and pets respect your professional space and not interfere with the conduct of your business.

A colleague of ours remembers getting a sales call from a woman who announced that she was a certified public accountant with a unique and highly valuable, professional service to offer her clients. Unfortunately, her phone presentation was obscured by the tantrum-like screams of a small, highly "unprofessional" child. What started out, he told us, as an excellent and quite compelling sales approach was ruined. It was obvious to our friend that the caller desperately needed a place to conduct her business in private. Please, a home-based business is a *professional* enterprise in every sense of the word. Make it so for your business.

Before settling on a location for your home office, consider a couple of things: foot traffic, machine noise (think twice about putting your office next to the laundry room), ventilation, heating and cooling, location of telephone lines, electrical circuits and windows. Too often, people select a location for a home-based office that is secondary to uses by other family members. That's a credit to your sense of fairness and consideration, but before you make that kind of decision, think about how much time you will spend in that office during the months and years to come. Think about the *purpose* of that office. If you are going to be spending one-third or one-fourth of your waking hours in that environment – *earning your and your family's living* – it should be as comfortable and convenient a place as possible. Think, too, about different times of day and plan on avoiding conflict with other family members' routines.

A dear friend of ours once located his home-based office in a downstairs room of his two-story house. Unfortunately, the room had no windows. Although it was well-lighted and quite comfortable from most standpoints, and attractively decorated as well, his inability to see outside bothered him greatly. He felt closed in, inhibited and constrained. Soon, he couldn't wait to get out of his office and *go home*! He eventually moved out – not of his home, but of that room. It became a wood-working shop where now he spends only a few minutes at a time.

You'll do well to consider the frequency of the room's usage. Do you have a living room that's not being lived in? Do you have an easily convertible, attached garage that seldom has a car parked in it, half of which would make a great office? Do you have a den or library that is used one or two days a month, or only once in a while in the evening? How about a guest room that is used only during the holidays? Some attic spaces are perfect – but be aware of seasonal extremes in temperature. These are all workable home-office possibilities.

It isn't necessary to have an eight foot, mahogany desk, executive chair, four-drawer, oak filing cabinet and plush carpeting to start your home-based office. Until you can afford such luxuries, a simple chair, table and temporary cardboard file case will do quite nicely. Second-hand office furniture outlets exist in most cities and there are great bargains to be had in the local paper's classifieds and *Penny-savers*. If you need to go the low budget route, it's okay. You don't have to impress anyone. Buy only what you need to get the job done. Frills, and even conveniences, can come later. And they will, right along with the financial independence possible with your Network Marketing business.

One other thing. Your family members will have to accommodate your new location and your new routine. They may even have to make some sacrifices to make your home office a reality. Involving everyone in your decision-making process will make it much easier – and you'll probably get some great ideas from them as well. Once your family understands the reason for the change and what positive benefits it will mean for them, they will accept the idea with grace. If you're like most of us, when your family is behind you and truly supportive, there's *nothing* you can't accomplish.

**2. Selecting a name**. As an individual, you can begin simply with your name, followed by "Independent Distributor for 'XYZ' Company. "However, the name you choose for your business can be very, very important. So give it a lot of thought. Here's why.

You only get one chance to make a first impression. The name of your business is what most people see or hear *first*. Your name is what marketing experts refer to as your *position*. Positioning is the image you and your business have in the mind of the public. And it's in the mind that your name gets its first chance to create a customer.

A bad position can break a business – even a rich and powerful one. Would you buy a Xerox computer? Or how about an Exxon office system? Both of these Fortune 500 giants *lost* a fortune – because of poor *positioning*. Xerox *means* copiers. Exxon *means* gas and oil. Nobody wanted computers from either of them – even though their products were excellent! A good position cannot promise to make a business successful, but it will help tremendously. Shake 'n' Bake says it all, and so does Taster's Choice, to name just a few. Our recommendation is that you choose a name that gives your potential consumer a clear idea of what your company does *and* that you do it better than anybody else.

If you see the name "AAA Rubber Stamp Co.," for example, you have a good general idea of the kind of product line and services they have to offer. The triple A "rating" is a statement of best or top quality, too. On the other hand, if you see the name "AAA Enterprises," you don't have a clue as to what they do, and the three "A"s fall on unimpressed eyes and deaf ears. If possible, use your own name or a form of your name as a part of the business name. In some states, doing so may save you from having to file a DBA (which means **D**oing **B**usiness **A**s) with the secretary of state's office. In many states, for example, if your name is Henry Hopkins and you call your business Hopkins' Distribution Co. or Hopkins' Home Products, you will not have to file a DBA. Using your own name has other advantages: it's much less likely that someone else will have chosen your business name (which keeps you clear of both trademark infringement problems and expensive trademark registration fees and legal costs); and many people feel that if a person's name is a part of the company name, that company is less likely to engage in dishonest practices. A company with a real person's name has that person standing behind it – it's a company you can trust. That is how many people feel.

Please, don't be tempted to use only initials. The public grants the privilege to use initials to businesses when their fame and reputation deserve it. IBM was International Business Machines for years *before* we started calling them IBM. The same was true for GE and AT&T. Spell it out for now.

In any case, be sure you are aware of all the regulations in your state regarding filing a business name. If filing a DBA is necessary, be sure you do it before opening your business checking account. Some banks require a copy of the DBA filing before they will open an account for you. If you choose to incorporate (which we'll discuss in Chapter 12), the first part of the process is "clearing" the corporate name in your state. A bank may want a copy of these papers as well.

**3. Opening a business checking account** is very important. Most of the time, people in the Network Marketing business buy and sell products. In the beginning, they send a personal check to pay for those products, and when they sell them, they put the money back into their personal account and spend it for groceries or other needs. They may make a good profit, but they won't know how much, when, or from what source. What do most people do when they have money? They spend it.

If you are serious about your business, you need a separate business account. You will need that account for tax purposes, but opening a business checking account is also visible evidence of your commitment and your decision to go into business for yourself.

Don't waste money on fancy checks or checkbooks. The cheapest are often the best. If you have a business name, consult the bank officer handling your account about the way your name should appear on the account and on the checks themselves. Some states have requirements that your name be listed first, then the initials "d/b/a" (doing business as), followed by your business or company name. For example:

Bill Smith d/b/a Smith's Home Products
500 Main Street
Anytown, U.S.A.

Your bank officer will know how to handle this procedure. Incidentally, all banks are not created equal. Choose your bank with the same care with which you'd choose a car. Shop around. Kick the tires by comparing fees, services, and most important of all, compare personal *chemistry*. It will be important for you to establish your account with a bank that welcomes you and your small business. Look for a small, solvent bank or a local neighborhood branch of a *big*, solvent bank. Find a bank that will take the time to help you and that will provide you with business tools that will make your banking activities easier and support your growth. If you feel a little shy about this, if you have a "Gee, I'm not a big deal. I feel funny asking for so much of their time" attitude – just remember: *You're a Network Marketer.* That banker may be looking at a future millionaire – *you.*

**4. Get a business telephone** line installed. *Do not use your home phone* for business calls – unless you're a single person with a limited social life. Having a business number allows you to deduct the entire phone bill as a business expense. You will also get a free listing in the business section of the telephone directory and Yellow Pages, *which can be a very big plus.* Having a phone line dedicated to business use will help everyone (including yourself) to think of you in a business-like way.

An answering machine is a must for your business phone. The once-detested device is now generally accepted by business people and just about everybody else. Some models allow you to check your messages from an outside phone. If you plan to travel, get one of those. Also, get a machine that records the date and time of the incoming call as well as one that allows for longer messages. You don't want an important message to be cut short by a trigger-happy answering device.

An alternative is a good telephone answering service where your phone is answered by a "live" person. This is very professional and makes a great impression. It may be too expensive at first, but if it's affordable – do it.

The way you answer your business phone is important to your business start-up. First, give callers your business name. Then, tell them who is speaking. "Smith's Distribution Co. – this is Bill Smith," is a simple but professional way to answer your business phone. Please, don't be cute or clever. Be a pro and play it straight.

A clinical psychologist whom we know established his private practice in a home-based office. While his practice was new, he answered his own phone. He had all the right words, but his tone of voice was a real turn-off. To callers, he sounded as if he was angry that they had interrupted his busy day. This was not the impression he wanted to give at all! We took him aside one day to tell him about the feeling potential clients were getting when he answered the phone. He was truly shocked! He hadn't realized what kind of business impression he was making. If you suspect you might be giving the wrong impression, one trick is to put a smile on your face before you pick up the receiver to answer a call. You simply cannot sound angry with that smile on your face. It works every time!

If other members of your family answer your business phone for you, even occasionally, be sure they are instructed in the proper way you want them to respond. Also be sure they record your messages properly, so that you can respond to them promptly and correctly. Even relatively young children can be taught this important process. If you make a game of it, they'll quickly learn.

**5. Get a sales tax license** if necessary. If you buy products at wholesale and sell them to retail customers, your state may require you to collect, report and pay state sales taxes. In most states, the license is available from the state department of revenue.

If you live in a city of any significant size, it also may require a sales license or permit. Make sure you check all your local government entities in order to comply with their regulations for new businesses. Having a sales tax license may have some advantages. Some companies will require a copy of your sales tax license before you can make wholesale purchases for resale. Also, any item you purchase that you intend to re-sell should be bought without state sales tax. You'll need your tax number in lieu of paying that tax. And having a sales tax license further legitimizes your new business. (More about permits and licenses in Chapter Six.)

**6. Order a rubber stamp** with your business name, address and phone number on it, so that every brochure, flyer, order form or piece of correspondence is clearly marked as coming from you. Otherwise, you'll be giving out literature to people who won't know who to contact for more information or for placing orders.

**7. Set up files** for prospects, sales, follow-up, distributors, tax information, expense receipts, etc. Setting up files doesn't need to be an expensive or complicated proposition. Buy a box of manila folders and some 3 x 5 index cards with alphabetical dividers and a box to put them in. If money is a factor, you can go low budget and buy a temporary cardboard filing box, folders, index cards, plus dividers, all for under $25. If you want to go first class, you can spend a lot more, but don't get so involved in organizing yourself that you forget to set aside time *for work.*

**8. Join your local Chamber of Commerce** as soon as you can afford to. Not only will you learn first hand about what is happening and what *will* happen in your community, but also, most Chambers have mixers, meetings and business breakfasts that will give you an excellent opportunity to meet new people and to make many new business contacts.

**9. Read all company brochures**, training materials and information your sponsor and your company provide. There is a good reason why your Network Marketing company spends so much money developing training materials and providing these brochures. It is so you can learn from them and not have to *reinvent the wheel*. Starting your own business is hard enough without having to be a Network Marketing pioneer. Besides, if you did take this approach, you'd be 30 years too late! Become familiar with all your products. You can't easily sell something in Network Marketing – a product, a service or an idea – that you have not personally experienced and have genuine enthusiasm for. In this sharing and recommending business, *your personal experience* with the products and your company is of primary importance. You should be familiar with the benefits of both.

**10. Develop an action plan** and write it down. Set specific goals for your new business. Each goal you write down should have a desired result and a timetable for completing it. Have one plan for the first 30 days. Have another for the next six months. Have yet another for your first year. This kind of planning may be the *most important thing you do* in getting started. You cannot succeed without knowing where you are going or without having a benchmark or standard to measure your progress. These plans are not ideas carved on stone tablets. You'll need to revise them – *often*. There will be many unknowns, especially for your one year plan. Don't let that stop you! It's vital that you begin thinking about the future immediately. It will save you endless frustration in the months to come.

Some notes about planning and goals: Both goal setting and planning work best *backwards*. What we mean is, reach out into the future, as far ahead as your imagination can go, and set those long-term goals first. Now ask yourself, "What would be the step just before achieving this last goal?" Keep working backwards from there until you get to today. Then make that call or get ready for that meeting. And please remember, "It's not just how you plan your work – it's how you work your plan."

**11. Finally, develop daily routines** and disciplines to establish a business-like attitude and atmosphere. This may seem elementary, but it needs to become a part of your new mind set. If you previously worked for someone else, getting started in your own business may be difficult for you. There is no one to care whether you get to work on time. There is no one to nag you about getting a project, task or assignment completed. There is no one to review your performance – no one to scold you for a poor job or praise you for a good one. No one whose job it is to make sure you're motivated. No one, that is, *but you*. You must begin to fill all of those roles. Opportunity is one side of the coin. Responsibility is the other. Commitment is the key, discipline the tool. And if you ever get off track, simply pull out your goals sheet and read it over again.

Establish good work habits from day one. A great way to begin is to pick a time that your office opens each day – and be in it faithfully at that time. Treat your home and your office as two separate places that just happen to be in the same building. Don't mix activities between the two. If you are tempted to watch television or do an odd job around the house, delay those activities to the same times you did them when you were employed by someone else. Let your family and the business community know immediately that you mean business and intend to conduct yourself as a professional! By the way, our favorite practical definition of a professional is: someone who does what it takes to get the job done – whether he or she feels like it or not.

When you announce that you're getting started in your own business, you are telling the world that you are ready to accept new risks and new responsibilities. You're telling everyone you know that you are willing to work harder and smarter than ever to make your dreams come true. You are letting everyone know that you are going to be successful in your new endeavor *and that you mean business.*

Encourage and acknowledge yourself by developing a system of self-rewards. The rewards may be small – at least at first – but this system should be in place so that when you meet or exceed a goal, your self-reward is available to you immediately. For example, you might create a reward bank account solely for this purpose. Acknowledge yourself for little things at first – $1 for every phone call made, $5 for attending a meeting, $10 every time you give a presentation – no matter what the outcome. Two things will begin to happen. First, you quickly realize that you're rewarded for doing what you said you'd do – you've got discipline and integrity. Second, in a *very* short time, you'll have a couple of hundred dollars in your account – and it's all profit! Do whatever you want with the money. You earned it and you deserve it!

---

In the next chapter, we'll show you several tools that you can use to help you generate success for your new business.

# *Chapter 5*
# Organizing
# for Success

*Nothing beats having a disciplined
"work ethic" – except a simple
system that makes it easy and fun.*

# Organizing for Success

Your Network Marketing business will involve many aspects of your character. Both logic and emotion play important roles in your success. Emotion deals with your belief systems and your attitudes, and it affects your unconscious habits of thinking. Logic is more left-brain. It governs the rational approach to your business. Let us say this in advance – what you are going to learn here can change your life! It will affect much more than just your business. The dangling carrot of financial and personal freedom provides you with the motivation (emotion) you need to begin to organize (logic) your business. The success you experience in organizing your business then spills over into other areas of your life. Organizing your business and yourself is a key to your Network Marketing success.

Organization is made up of two complementary parts: efficiency and effectiveness. Efficiency – is doing things right. Effectiveness – is doing the right things. This chapter deals with both.

First, let's talk about organization itself. For many people, it's a favorite "denial" word. It brings up images of drudgery, boredom and outside limits imposed on their creative flow. "Organization" means *to form into a whole of interdependent or coordinated parts for harmonious or united action.* Organize comes from the Greek, *organ,* which means: "implement, tool, bodily organ or musical instrument." It's a close cousin of the Greek word *ergon,* which means "work."

You can see, from these definitions and derivations, that organization has much to do with being a tool you use to accomplish things, much like the telephone or computer you use. It's also natural (as in *organic*) and has a direct connection to *musical instruments*. Organization, like playing music, does require discipline. The result of organization is *harmonious or united action*. We don't know anybody who doesn't want that – especially for their business.

## Why Get Organized?

Getting organized in business allows you to transform potential assets into opportunities for action. In other words – work into money. For example, if you have a stack of sales prospects but no organization in your filing system, you simply will not be effective. You may not want to hear this. You may be the kind of person who thrives on _dis_organization. You know, the kind of person who used to have a sign on your desk that read: "A cluttered desk is a sign of a busy mind"– if only you could remember where you put it! You like it that way.

Well, if you really do thrive on clutter, that's all right with us. We're not going to ask you to clear everything off your desk, unless the clean-desk system happens to work better for you. But we are going to show you various ways to put a monthly commission check on top of your desk – cluttered or uncluttered. What you do with it then is your business. Just make sure you remember where you put it!

## Time *Is* on Your Side

Wouldn't it be great if we could learn new skills in a single afternoon? What would it be worth to you if in one afternoon – just a few hours – you could learn how to type a hundred words a minute, without making a mistake? What would it be worth to you if you could master a modern word processing system in an afternoon? Would you pay $100? $500? We would. But this is the real world, so it takes practice, time, dedication and some degree of physical dexterity to achieve such a useful goal.

We probably could do it, *if we had the time*. We all know it would be great if we could type at lightning speed. Those of us who don't type well know that we ought to learn how to type, but we just don't have enough time or patience. We're already much too busy to spend time learning how to type at this late date, so we just struggle along hunting and pecking. This is the same problem that successful salespeople face when their selling skills overtake their organizational skills. They think it is too late to learn. So they struggle along, always wishing they had organized everything right from the beginning – *when they had the time*.

What does typing have to do with your business? Are we going to ask you to type up lists of your prospects? Absolutely not – *but we are* going to ask you to devote the time necessary to set up a filing system for your prospects and for your business, because it eventually will increase your effectiveness tenfold. You may not feel that this is necessary at first, but we guarantee that looking frantically for just one lost prospect card will consume more time later on than organizing your files takes today.

You see, you really *always have time*. Time is already, always present – right here, right now. You simply have to *make* time. So, *make* the time to get organized now, while you *have* the time to learn. Like a monthly investment program, a little bit invested now pays greater and greater dividends the longer you stick with the program.

## What You'll Need

If you don't have the necessary supplies, go to an office supply store, college book store or some other discount store that has a selection of office supplies, and buy the following:

1. **A business card file.** This is usually a small plastic box designed to hold several hundred business cards. It will come complete with dividers. Or you may choose a folder with plastic pages that will hold your card collection.

2. **A large pack of 3 X 5 cards, alphabet dividers and a box** to hold them. This will become your prospect file.

3. **A package of dividers** numbered 1-31, and another for each month of the year. This will become your "Business Manager in a Box"

4. **A box of 100 manila file folders.**

5. **A cardboard file box** – if you don't already have a filing cabinet or drawer.

Your total investment is less than $25, and you now have all the items necessary for success in organizing your prospects and other business files.

## Setting Up a Business Card File

Now, go through your wallet, your desk drawers, dresser drawers, glove compartment, briefcase, car trunk and any other place you might have tucked away somebody's business card. Put every single one in your business card file. You may decide to file them alphabetically by last name, by profession, by the name of the company, or by the name of the friend who gave you the referral. Any system that works for you is fine – just use a system!

Before you file the cards, make any notations on the front or back of them that would help you remember an opening for the people who gave you the card, or any conversation that might give you a lead-in for presenting your product and business opportunity to them. Write down the date and place you met –whether it was at the office, in a home or at a social event. Include any information you can use to help you establish rapport the next time you contact that person. Write down whatever you think might help you to remember him or her, or anything memorable about their office, home or family. The smaller you write, the better.

File the cards in a way that will help you think of that person when you start looking for his or her card. If you would normally think of a person as a dentist rather than by his or her name, file the card under "D" for dentist. Keep all of your business cards together in this handy little box or folder. Make a habit of putting them there the moment you get one. Don't let them lie forgotten in your wallet. Business cards represent potential money – don't lose them!

When you file the cards, most of these people will be "cold" or "lukewarm" prospects. They just exist, and at this point you have no idea whether or not they are going to be interested in your product and business opportunity. Later, when you start working with this referral box, you can move some of these cards to your prospect file.

## Setting Up a Prospect File

Use your blank 3 x 5 cards to set up your prospect file. On these cards put basic information about each person you talk to about your product or about going into business with you. Always include his or her name, address and phone number on the upper left or right hand corner of the card. If they use a business card, get two from them: staple one to the 3 x 5 card and file the other.

Also, you should make notations on this card about the date and place of each contact with every individual. Not only will this refresh your memory, but you also can use this information to help each person you contact remember you when you call and say, "Hi, Bill, this is…" If Bill can't remember who *you* are, remind him of the date and place where you last met. You might even tell him right up front, so he won't have to be embarrassed to admit he doesn't remember you.

One very important thing you'll need to include on this card is information about what you consider to be the person's "motivation factor" – that is, his or her need for your product and business opportunity. Maybe Bill told you he has a dead end job, or that he has kids who will be going to college in two years. Find out his needs and wants, and note them on the card so you can address these concerns during your next contact with him.

If this person works in a company or profession that screens telephone calls or makes it very difficult to contact him personally, make a notation of the receptionist's or secretary's name or the key person who can make sure your call will get through. Knowing the names of a person's staff members and associates can be a most valuable asset when you make your next call.

Obviously, the best time to get this information is when the person first hands you his or her card. Everyone likes to talk about himself – it's just a question of whether or not *you* are the right kind of person to talk to – so be a good listener. Ask questions. Be genuinely interested. And that's easy to do, because you *are* interested! Get all the information you can. Write small. Some day, you may even want to computerize all this information, but that's down the road.

You can divide these cards into "hot" prospects and "lukewarm" prospects, or use any other division that meets your needs. Obviously, you should contact the hot prospects first – *before* they cool off. Review your cards on a regular basis. Check to see when you had your last contact with each person. Decide when you will contact them next, and put their card under that date in your "Manager in a Box" file (more on that in a moment). Try to think of a new way to approach them on the subject. Each of us has different moods and attitudes on any given day, and sometimes people change a number of times during the same day. Maybe you just caught someone at a bad time before, or maybe conditions have changed in his or her life, so that they would be more receptive to hearing about your product or opportunity now.

Always leave the door open. Successful Network Marketing is about: "Saying the right things – to the right people – at the right time." If your prospect isn't interested today, ask him directly if you can keep in touch, then give him a call back in a month or so just to ask how he's doing and to let him know how you're doing. A "yes" answer to this request gives you permission to get back in touch with him. Put his card behind that date in your file. We can't count how many times a "not interested" has turned into "I'm interested" just a few weeks or months down the road. This is especially true as your success grows. So always share your success with your prospects, and leave the door open. Timing is the key.

Keep making notes on the cards about your contacts, follow-up activities and any encouraging results you received. Your next contact may be the one during which they say, "Yes, I'm interested."

## Using Your "Manager in a Box"

A "Manager in a Box" is just that. It's a simple physical system that acts just like having a personal office manager for your business – and will save you about $49,995 a year in salary! It's a systematic reminder file which is kept by day of the month and month of the year. You will have a section for each month and one for each day of the month – days 1-31. Place the name of the current month in front of the numbers for the days of that month. At the end of each month, move the name of the past month to the back of the file and the new month to the front of your numbered files.

The purpose of the "Manager in a Box," which people also call a "tickler file," is to "tickle" or "jog" your memory about who you are supposed to see or call that day or that month. If you meet with Max in July, and he tells you, "Contact me in a couple of months," he probably assumes that you will forget to contact him. Boy, will he be surprised! In preparation for Max's Surprise Day, go back to your office and place a note in the September file to contact Max. "Hello, Max, this is… You asked me to call you back in a couple of months, so I thought I'd follow through today." Take September's list of all the people you are supposed to call – then divide the list by the days on which you will contact each person.

This technique is not only very effective for people you need to see, but also things you need to get done. It is an excellent place to record birthdays, anniversaries and other special occasions you tend to forget. Make it a habit to check your tickler file each day to see what you need to do on that day and the next day. Use your system. Once you make it a habit, you will realize how effective and powerful it is, and you will do it effortlessly and automatically. It will help you manage your time, your business and your life – and all for $5 and just minutes a day! Your "Manager in a Box" will become invaluable.

## Setting Up Alphabetical Files

Next, you need to set up alphabetical files. Using manila file folders, start grouping your important papers by topic and filing them alphabetically.

- Set up files for each of your distributors.
- Set up files for your meetings.
- Set up files for your training materials.
- Set up files for your important papers.
- Set up files for your receipts and tax records.

- Set up files for all your current projects.
- Set up files for your car and equipment titles.
- Set up files for your car mileage and expenses.
- Set up files for your warranties and guarantees.
- Set up a "DONE" file – that's a "To Do" file with a positive attitude!
- Set up files for family members, health records and other important personal papers.
- Set up files on anything you need to keep and refer to occasionally.
- And, set up a Big Idea file, too!

It is amazing how many people do not have a filing system – even for their household documents. Not only would it be an extremely helpful thing for your family in the event of an emergency, but it could actually prolong your life by reducing the considerable tension and stress involved in spending hours or days searching for a document that should be right at your fingertips.

Put your file folders in your cardboard file box if you don't have a filing cabinet or drawer.

---

In this chapter, we have given you some very simple, inexpensive and easy to use tools to help you stay on top of your business. Of course, we can't *make* you do it, but it will become obvious to the others who deal with you whether or not you are organized and on top of your business. And of course, don't do it for them – certainly don't do it for us – *do it for yourself and your successful business!*

It's been our experience that anyone who has gone to the trouble of setting up some kind of filing system is serious about being in business. Getting organized is the first step in getting your business life under control. It's also an important initial step for achieving business success. Now, you really do have an incentive to get organized. Investing time and effort into your business is just like investing money – and in many ways, your return will be much greater. Keep your business organized by using these easy filing, storage and retrieval tools. The benefits will far outweigh the costs. And, of course, it's all tax-deductible!

## Chapter 6
# How to Be a Success

*How to develop a Million Dollar*
*Attitude – Listening and Teaching*
*your way to success*

# How to Be a Success

**W**hat it takes for starters is: the power of a *truly* positive attitude. It's important for you to grow personally as your organization grows. In fact, your personal growth comes, more often than not, *prior to the success of your organization*. Both you and your Network Organization must be in dynamic, harmonious balance. Otherwise, like a heavy person and a skinny person sitting at opposite ends of a teeter-totter, it's hard to develop any positive and continuous momentum to get things done.

Expanding your self-image will help tremendously with your prospecting. It will enable you to develop what we call a "Million Dollar Attitude." A Million Dollar Attitude is the key to success in this business of Network Marketing. Unfortunately, many times people assume a "10¢ attitude" – or what's sometimes called – an "alligator mentality."

Suppose you went over and knocked on your neighbor's door and said, "Neighbor, I'm so excited, I've got to share this with you... This is just the greatest thing I have ever run into... You've just got to see this... I love it!... It's a fantastic product... I'm going to make $5,000 a month – $60,000 a year in a business of my own!"

Then what happens? All of a sudden, he or she suddenly develops huge, sharp teeth and attacks immediately, ripping the meat of happiness and expectation right off your bones. Your neighbor begins to talk like an alligator: "Don't you know anything – 85 percent of the people that go into business for themselves don't make it the first year. Do you want to go bankrupt? Some of my wife's-sister's-boyfriend's-mother's girlfriends got into a deal like that – and they still have a garage load of junk they can't give away. Boy, are they sorry they ever got involved with that."

Or your helpful neighbor might say, "We've been friends for years and I've never told you this before, but just to save you money and heartache, this time I will – you're just not the entrepreneurial type. Besides, if that scheme really worked, don't you think I'd be into it, too? Nooo, not me. I'm not *that* stupid!"

Often these kinds of comments are offered out of genuine concern. So, don't write off everybody who talks alligator as all being bad guys. By calling them "alligators," we're referring to the snapping, negative attitude, which is actually a defense. These people usually are stuck in their comfort zone. You don't see a lot of activity for change out of them – risk taking of any kind just isn't their style. But you sure get their attention whenever you show them your energy and enthusiasm. If they cannot identify with what you are offering, a negative response is not unusual. It may be that they haven't had a good sense of their own worth for so long that your enthusiasm actually scares them. Let that be okay. They have their experience and opinions – and you have yours.

When someone says that he or she really isn't interested, accept that answer for the moment. But don't think a negative response means that you've hit a dead end. Remember, *timing is the key*. In a week, or a month, that person might be more open to considering what you have to offer. Especially when they begin to see how successful you're becoming. As we said before, always leave the door open if you can.

One way to do this is to ask that person for references. You can say something like this: "I know it takes time and energy to be successful in Network Marketing. And I'm committed to doing it. Maybe you know someone in your family or at work who might be interested in experiencing the benefits of my products and making a few hundred extra dollars each month as well. Would you be willing to give me the names of anyone you know at work who you think might be a good prospect for me? What about someone in your family, or one of your friends?"

You'll probably get some solid referrals by using this approach. At the same time, you'll be subtly reminding that person of all the contacts he or she already knows. You'll be on "public record" as being determined to become a success, and that's a big plus for your own self-esteem. You'll also be letting that person know that there are real benefits to be experienced with your products and real money to be made in Network Marketing – if he or she ever does choose to get involved.

You could also follow up with something like this: "I don't want to take future prospects away from you. I'll make you a deal. If I sponsor anyone as a result of your recommendation, I'll turn them over to you for your own Network Organization – if you sign up within 30 days after I let you know I've sponsored them. How's that?" You'll most likely find this person much more open to what you have to offer the second time around.

## You Just Never Know

People are all different. You'll never really be able to know who will respond favorably to your product or opportunity. The best thing to do is to assume *everybody's* a great prospect. No matter what, you will always have to deal with some people who aren't interested – *yet!* There is no way to avoid this problem with anything that is worth sharing with people. In other words, you *are* going to experience rejection. Accept that this is inevitable, and you will be able to react positively.

Some prospects may not be ready for it, but if they recognize that you're really enthusiastic and that you have their best interests at heart, they won't be offended. Realize that some people don't have the same vision or share the same concerns that you do. This is natural and normal. Others may share your vision and concerns, but have chosen other ways to achieve their goals. This is normal, too.

You may be thinking, "I don't want to alienate people who aren't yet interested, but I do want to get the story out to those who really are." You don't know which are which. However, one thing is certain – you must be fully persuaded and enthused that your product and program is a good one, that you really believe in it, and that you know that it's worth working for in order to achieve your goals.

What you want to do, is to develop a...

## Million Dollar Attitude

A Million Dollar Attitude cannot be shaken, regardless of what happens. A good example of that comes from an old TV program called *The Millionaire.*

A billionaire named John Baresford Tipton was interested in human nature and human reactions. What he did was to give away, tax-free, a cashier's check for $1 million to people he selected at random, and then watch what happened to them. His secretary was a man named Michael Anthony; it was his job to go around and give out the million-dollar checks. He certainly had a great product! He was offering something you would think everyone in the world would want. But there was one episode in which Michael Anthony knocked on the door and the guy inside said, "I don't care what you are selling or what you are going to give me. I don't want it. Go away!" and slammed the door right in Michael's face.

Has that ever happened to you when you were trying to share something?

Did the rejection change Michael Anthony's attitude? Did it change his self-image or self-worth in any way? No, not at all. Michael just smiled and was persistent. He had a job to do – to give away a million dollars – and he was committed to following through. Finally, when "his prospect" fully understood the opportunity that was being presented to him, Michael was welcomed in with open arms.

How different is what you have to offer from what Michael Anthony was giving people? We've met many successful distributors over the years, and most of them say the person who sponsored them into Network Marketing was just like Michael Anthony. The products and the opportunity he or she gave them was just like a check for $1 million. It just wasn't tax-free.

This is the same attitude, the same conviction that each of us needs to develop for the business that we're in. This is what will give you the energy and the power to build your Network Organization consistently – not just this month, but this year, and next year and in the years to come. Perhaps 10 years from now, you can take a break if you want – but you probably won't want to.

Simply put, a Million Dollar Attitude is one where you *know*, beyond a shadow of a doubt, that the products or service you're offering, the business opportunity and the company you represent, are *worth $1 million* to everyone you share them with. Now, with an attitude like that – what are your chances for Network Marketing success?

## Secrets of Good Communication

Let's look at what makes for good communication. Why take the time? Because effectively communicating with others is vital to building and maintaining a successful Networking Organization.

Think of it this way: in the human body, it's blood that makes the whole thing work. It's blood that brings oxygen and nutrition to each one of your trillion or so cells. It's blood that carries energy to the various parts of the body, such as organs and muscles. Blood protects the body against disease and keeps it vital and strong. It's the quality of your blood that determines your health and your life. In a Network Organization, *communication* is its life's blood.

People are motivated by knowing *how* to achieve their goals. Only through good communication – speaking *and* listening – can we understand exactly what it is they want to achieve. Then we can communicate to them the steps they can take to achieve them.

Listening is, of course, the foundation to good communication. The better we are at "really hearing" what the other person has to say, the more effective we will be at showing them how to get what they want.

Also, remember that perfect transmission does not insure perfect reception. It has been said that three-quarters of what we hear goes in one ear and right out the other. One reason for this is that the mind can hear and accept from three to four hundred words per minute. Yet even a person who seems to be talking very fast generally speaks only from 100 to 125 words per minute. What this means is that you have the capacity to hear every word that is being said, but at the same time, your attention actually can be focused somewhere else.

If, for example, you and a friend were in the middle of a conversation in which the word "boat" came up, and this brought to your mind the last time you were out on a lake fishing or water-skiing, you might find that you're doing more reminiscing or day dreaming about the past than you are listening at that moment. Yet, you could say that you are hearing every word. But are you? There is hearing – and then there is *hearing*.

To really understand what the other person is trying to communicate, you must hear more than his or her words. We don't always – and perhaps only rarely – say all that is on our minds in the form of words. The way to overcome this as a listener is to look for ways to connect everything the person is saying to ways of achieving his or her ultimate goal or purpose. You need to understand people's goals in order to show them how you will help meet those goals for them. Paying close attention to everything that is said, whether or not you agree with it, will contribute directly to the achievement of *your* goals. Whether it's sooner or later will depend on how well you really listen, and how well you can relate what you hear to the product benefits and opportunity you are presenting.

## The Secret Is Simple

The secret of success in a sales business is simple – although it takes time to really learn. You show someone how to achieve his or her goals by encouraging him or her to purchase what you are selling – you have them try the product or service themselves. Then you motivate him or her to take decisive action and follow through on what he or she already believes – sharing the benefits they've experienced using the product. Knowledge without action is useless. It is not enough to be a *knower* of the truth; a person must become a *doer*. You help him or her to do both. This is the salesperson's three-fold task: *to listen, to teach*, and *to motivate*.

One key to good communication is to let people say what they have to say – in their own way. If you try to get people to use *your* words, they soon will stop listening and talking with you. When they stop talking about their goals and dreams, your job becomes impossible, because your job *is* to help them achieve those goals and dreams.

The only way you can really discover how to help, lead and guide people is for them to share what's really important to them. Sometimes, we may think we are in control of a situation because we're doing the talking. However, if the other person has something important on her mind that she has not been able to express, she may not hear a word you say.

You not only want to listen, but you also want to concentrate on what is being said. In other words, don't let your mind wander when the other person is talking. Don't be thinking about what you are going to say next. The key is to practice being an "open listener." It's simple really: *simply* be open to what's being said. Suspend your judgments, editorializing or comments and don't think anything about what you hear. That's *really* listening. Trust that you'll know what to say when your turn comes. The truth is – you will.

Don't feel badly about taking notes when somebody else is talking. You can't remember everything. In fact, trying to remember what was just said blocks out what's being said *at this moment*. Truth is, most people are impressed when someone cares enough to write down what they are saying. Maybe you won't think of the perfect answer this time, but if you have a few notes on what your prospective customer or distributor has said, you can think of solutions later on. You will be surprised how ready people are to tell you about their hopes and dreams. We also suggest that if you're making a note about an important point, ask the speaker to stop while you make it. If you're writing notes, you can't be really listening. A tape recorder can be a big help here, especially in a meeting with lots of people. Let the machine do the remembering for you. Then you can concentrate on listening and being "fully present ."

Also, if what someone says is contrary to your understanding of what is best – don't cut them off. Let them fully express their thoughts and feelings. If you give people your full attention, later on they will be far more likely to give you theirs. This will avoid a lot of pre-judging and "wishful hearing" on everyone's part. Again, the key is being an "open listener."

When you discuss something, especially something new to either of you, make sure you understand the meaning of the words that are used. The same words will mean different things to different people. These can be fairly common words that we use often or they can be industry "buzz words." If either you or the person you're speaking to are not sure about the meaning of something, stop right there and clear it up. This will prevent everyone from jumping to conclusions. If you think a lot of explanation may hinder the conversation, then avoid buzz words in the first place. For example, mentioning your "downline" may be meaningful to you, but may mean absolutely nothing to the person with whom you are trying to communicate.

Remember, the other person isn't really interested in the fine details of every aspect of your product or program. What he or she is interested in is finding out a believable way to achieve his or her goals. The newcomer to Network Marketing is like a person who doesn't care how to fix a broken piece of equipment. They just want to know if the product really will get results *for them* – if the program really will work – *for them*. If the person gets too confused, he or she will "turn off." It's a natural response to prevent overload. So don't try to tell them everything all at once. Focus on the benefits for them – not all the features and technical details.

## Ask, Ask, Ask – Then Ask Some More

Perhaps the most important thing you can do in good communication – next to listening – is to ask questions. Many people do not automatically volunteer everything that is on their minds or that they're feeling. They may not be aware of some important problem or concerns. If you think of something that is pertinent to the subject you are discussing, or something that would help you understand how to ask a better question, then listen. Sometimes we have information stored away mentally without really knowing what it means.

By asking questions and discussing things, everyone will have a better understanding of what is going on. The Greek philosopher, Plato, said the truth was revealed in dialogue. He was right – listen to him!

## A Good Exercise

For those of you who want to hold organized training sessions as you build your distributor organization, let us give you a good exercise to try:

First, have everyone pair off, preferably with someone they don't know well. Have one person ask the other what it is they would like to achieve with their business. Then let the questioner listen for two full minutes. When the two minutes are up, they change roles and repeat the exercise. After everyone has had his or her turn, have each person stand up and share with the group what they have learned *about their partner*. Before you start this exercise, explain what they will be asked to do. It will bring everyone's total attention to what they're doing and will create a sense of shared purpose within the group. Most of them will be surprised how much they learn, and how much easier it is to stand up and talk about someone else than it is to talk about themselves. Explaining the program also will be much easier for everyone after this exercise. And there's a marvelous side benefit too: everyone present will have had the direct experience of being a successful speaker and leader!

## Telling the Story

Remember, you are in a business that depends on your ability to "tell the story." Sharing the benefits of the product line and working with others to teach them to tell *their* own stories is what Network Marketing is all about. This means you must learn to tell that special part of your company's story that meets the needs of each individual you talk to.

Every person will have a slightly different set of needs, so you want to be able to spot what aspect of the business to tell them about. Then, tell them the story.

You may say, or someone may say to you, "I'm just not a salesperson. I can't talk to everyone the way you do, let alone stand up and lead a group." That may be true *for now*. However, if you experience any benefits from a product or a program, you share this personal testimony with others anyway – sales or no sales. Recommending something that we are excited about ourselves is only natural. Everybody does it. Just think of a great place to eat you know about... or a good book, a kind of car that excites you, a pen, lawn mower, perfume, soap... truth is, you can't stop yourself from sharing a good thing with other people. And all you have to do – after you share your personal recommendation with someone – is to ask, "Can you see a benefit in this for you?" And then, of course, *listen*.

People wonder why Network Marketing companies experience so much success by taking people with no experience in selling and making "professional salespeople" out of them. Here's the secret: Successful Network Marketing companies have a legitimate and exciting story to tell. Distributors simply tell the story and encourage others to do the same. This is why most companies spend so much money to produce effective brochures and sales aids to help tell the story for you. What you do is add your personal experience.

All you really need to get started is the enthusiasm that comes from the belief you have in what you are sharing. It is *the story you have to tell* that gives you the power to be effective and successful.

## Extroverts versus Introverts

Let's get rid of a myth accepted by many people as "the truth about salespeople." Many people believe that the most successful sales people are extroverts, that they have a natural gift of gab. Or, "Successful salespeople are those who are outgoing – the proverbial *life of the party.*" While these personality traits may help some folks to sell, these extroverts *are not* in the majority when it comes to superstar status in the sales world. *Far from it!*

One study we know about may be of particular interest to you. A survey of salespeople who consistently earned over $100,000 per year indicated by their own admission that more than 80 percent of them were introverts! They were people who would much rather read a book, go for a quiet walk or just be by themselves, rather than be with a group of people. Yet, when it came to selling their products or services, they were just as enthusiastic as anyone, if not more so. Why? Because *they really believed in the benefits* they were sharing with others. (Remember that Million Dollar Attitude). Also, they were much better prepared than most. Since they felt as though they didn't have a natural knack for selling or communicating, they studied more, worked harder and simply put more effort into communicating than most extroverts, who relied on personality instead of preparation to communicate the benefits of their products to others.

People who seldom have anything to say often come alive all of a sudden with energy and power in order to share something they care about with others. They do it without a thought about themselves, because they really believe in what they are doing. If you have that kind of enthusiasm about your product and your business, you *will be successful!* That's a promise. Your genuine enthusiasm, flowing forth from an inner resource of conviction, is the most powerful creative ability you possess. Everything else about your business can be learned and put into practice with time and effort on your part. In other words, it's all down-hill from here.

Introvert or extrovert – or somewhere in between – if you take the time to listen carefully and communicate with others in this business, you will find that you will experience more personal growth, become more personally and professionally empowered and empowering for others, and enjoy Network Marketing more than any other career you could pursue.

---

Now that you know what it takes to be a success, let's begin to apply what you've learned to the business of our business. In Network Marketing, "where the rubber meets the road" is *The Product*. That's what our next chapter is all about.

# *Chapter 7*
# Your Product
# or Service

*What's the cornerstone of Network
Marketing Success?  Being your
own best customer.*

# Your Product or Service

There are two ways to earn money as a Network Marketing distributor – through *sponsoring* other distributors and through *retailing*.

## Sponsoring

By sponsoring friends and associates into your Network as distributors and training them to retail the product (and whenever we say "product," please take that to include "services" as well) and sponsor others, you can develop a Network Sales Organization and receive overrides or bonus commissions on all the sales generated by that organization. Some of the most successful distributors have achieved financial independence through this unique feature of Network Marketing.

## Retailing

Whether or not you decide to develop a Network of distributors, there are profits aplenty to be made by retailing your product. This is called "Direct Selling." To retail, you simply share information about the benefits of your product and the sales that result from that sharing can amount to substantial profits for you.

Although retailing and sponsoring are the two sides of the Network Marketing coin, we assert that retailing comes first. And the most important ingredient in retailing is *the product*! Here's why.

## The Driving Force

You and your Network of distributors could be called the driving force of your Network Marketing Company. What we mean by "Driving Force" is "...*the primary determiner of the scope of future products and markets*." According to management gurus Benjamin Tregoe and John Zimmerman, of Kepner Tregoe, Inc. (authors of *Top Management Strategy*, Simon & Schuster, New York), a company's driving force is the basis upon which all strategic decisions are made. So, for the Network Marketing company you work with, giving you what *you* need to succeed – structure, support, compensation, distribution, services, etc. – is the most important factor of their business. Your company will succeed in direct proportion to the extent that you and your Network of Distributors are successful. In short, a good Network Marketing Company is *distributor driven* – i.e., your business well-being must be the basis upon which they base the actions of the company. *You* are their most important concern.

So, what's the driving force for *your* independent contractor business? We say your business is "product driven." Here's why.

## Your Ideal Business, Revisited

Remember in Chapter Three, *Your Ideal Business*, we listed eight elements your business requires for success? Well, if you look back, you'll see that every one of those points dealt to some extent with the product. Your Ideal Business should:

**Sell The World.** Both the marketplace and the product itself should be as "universal" as possible. That means, you want an excellent product that appeals to a vast (and preferably growing) number of consumers.

**Be in Demand.** A life enhancing product is a must, a "life changing" product is even better. The greater the demand for your product, the better your potential success. In short, people have to want your product – whether they know it or not.

**Serve a Continuing Demand.** This means a "consumable" product. Although a one time sale may be lucrative, a sale each month, month after month, is far and away the best.

**Have Low Overhead and Low Investment.** You don't want your money tied up in excess product inventory. A consumable product that's in demand will "turn over" rapidly, which means every month you should sell just about all the product you have in stock. Even better is when your distributors deal directly with the company. That way the company – not you – holds and pays for their inventory.

**Offer Special Products.** This is much more than a "given." Having unique, excellent products which are rarely (if ever) available from any other source, is one key that makes Network Marketing itself so special. Many of the products you'll find in our business are of the one-of-a-kind, leading edge type. Normal channels of sales and distribution simply cannot sell special products as effectively as Network Marketing can. That's because there's a higher education factor to special products, and they're best sold by people sharing with others their own enthusiasm and the benefits they've actually experienced themselves.

**Be a Cash Business.** You don't want to be a banker. And that's what you are if you sell something you've already paid for and have to wait until your customer pays you. Network Marketing is a money up-front or COD (Cash On Delivery) business. This also means that when you sell a product to a retail customer, you get paid your commission on that sale right then and there.

**Be Legal.** Your company has already done all that's necessary to provide you with a product that meets all the legal requirements for ingredients, packaging, etc. However, there is one area of concern for independent distributors. You *cannot* make claims about your product if those claims aren't legally supported. For instance, many products which are classified as "foods" may have an impact on a person's health. You can make "medical" claims for certain "drugs," but not for food products. For foods, the only thing you can legally claim is what is known to be true with respect to the product's nutritional content. For example, "such and such is high in Vitamin C." But you *do* have a right to share *your personal experience.*

Many Network Marketing companies offer products that actually make a real and positive difference in how people feel, look and even think. Some people have experienced truly remarkable, life-changing results from the products they use. Although you are prohibited from making medical claims, and you can't get up in large public gatherings and go on and on and on, you are allowed to share your own experience directly, one-on-one with another person. And if you think a product has done fantastic things for you, sharing these benefits with friends and family through your personal testimonial is the most powerful sales tool imaginable. It's one reason for the great success of many products sold through Network Marketing that simply could not be sold effectively any other way.

Now you see how the product itself is an integral part of your ideal business – why do we consider it the force that drives your business?

## Retailing Is the Key

You may have heard the old line about the first three ingredients for a successful retail store are, "Location, location and location." In Network Marketing, the three ingredients are, "Retail, retail and retail." Here's why.

Look at what happens with almost every "satisfied customer" of any product or service. Someone (with a personal recommendation) or something (such as an ad on TV) initially communicates the benefits of a product to someone... that person tries it... they get good results... and then, they share the benefits and their satisfaction with the product with others. It's natural. It happens all the time. If you discover a great restaurant, see a terrific movie or really love the car you drive or the shampoo you use, you share your enthusiasm for that "product" with other people. Just imagine if you'd been paid a couple of dollars for every product you'd ever recommended to anybody who tried it and liked it. And just imagine if they kept coming back and buying it again and again, month after month – and each time, you got paid again. Incredible! Now, what Network Marketing companies do is to offer all of us the opportunity to be rewarded for successfully sharing their products personally with other people. When you get paid for successfully sharing products with people – you're selling.

In Network Marketing, retailing is when you sell your product directly to someone. You earn a commission on that retail sale, because you buy the product at the wholesale price from the company and sell it for a higher retail price to your customer. The difference between the wholesale cost you pay and the retail selling price your customer pays you is your retail sales commission. In an exclusively Direct Selling business, those commissions are how you earn your income.

But Network Marketing adds another "profitable" dimension. Many of your retail customers will, just like you, recommend the products to others. Some of them will immediately see doing what you do – making retail sales – as an attractive business proposition. Others, will, over time, discover that they, too, could be earning additional income by successfully recommending and retailing the products. These people you will sponsor into the business by making them part of your Distributor Network Organization. Then you will receive commissions on the retail sales they make and on the retail sales made by people they sponsor as well. The key element in all of this is retail sales.

Retail sales are vital in Network Marketing for the following reasons:

**1. Retailing pays you for your time.** You should make a reasonable retail profit when you sell products to your customers. Exclusive of the multiple level commissions you earn from the sales made by the distributors in your Network, your own retail sales must compensate you for your time with a good hourly wage.

**2. Retailing is prospecting for your Network.** The vast majority of the men and women who join your Distributor Sales Network will come from your retail customer base. The more you retail, the more prospective distributors you'll have, and the more your Network will grow. Continual retailing is the key to a long-lasting, constantly growing, profitable Network Marketing business.

**3. Retailing is the key to a big income.** As the leader of your Network, the people you sponsor will do what you do. If all you do is sponsor new people, *without* retailing the product, you'll end up with a big downline group with little total sales volume and no real income. If, on the other hand, everyone in your Network actively retails, *just the way you do,* your total group volume and the commissions you earn from those sales will be quite substantial.

For example: Let's say you have 100 people in your organization (those you've directly sponsored and the people they've sponsored as well). And let's assume that each of them uses $50 worth of wholesale product per month themselves, yet doesn't retail to others. Your total group sales volume would be $5,000 ($100 x 50). If your override commissions averaged 10 percent, you would earn about $500 per month. Now, if each of those people were actively retailing just one $50 order every two weeks in addition to their own purchases, that would be an extra $100 per distributor per month in sales volume – a total of $15,000 in sales and your commission would be $1,500. That difference could buy you a house!

**4. Retailing is also a concern for regulatory agencies.** If a Network Marketing company's retail presence in the marketplace is slight or non-existent, it may become an issue for the states' attorneys general. One of their offices' primary concerns is to protect consumers against illegal pyramid schemes and chain letter type operations. One thing these unethical "opportunities" have in common is that they pay people *for the act of recruiting*. That's not legal. A legitimate Network Marketing company *offers valuable products* through its independent distributors, and those distributors, in turn, offer and sell those products to retail customers. The only way the distributor earns income – whether directly (through retailing) or indirectly (through commissions and bonuses) – is on the sales of those products. (It should be noted that many leading companies and regulatory agencies recognize as a retail sale purchases by distributors in reasonable amounts for personal or family use.)

So, retailing is the key to your successful Network Marketing business – and "the product" is the key to retailing. What's important about the product?

## In Network Marketing, the Product Is King (or Queen)

As we said in the beginning of this chapter, you earn money in two ways; sponsoring and retailing. We've pretty thoroughly explained how retailing generates income for your business, and how the people you sponsor into your Sales Network earn money for you based on their retail sales. There are just a few additional important points to mention.

Sometimes, people are attracted to a Network Marketing business opportunity based on a great compensation plan, on fantastic promotional ideas or dynamic marketing techniques. Don't misunderstand us, these things are wonderful and if your company does them for you – that's great! *BUT*, none of these elements, nor any other "business opportunity" feature, no matter how exciting or initially productive for you, is a foundation upon which to build your business. Why? Because, like being the fastest gun in the West, there is always somebody out there who's just a little bit faster. If you sponsor someone into your Network Marketing business based on the money making opportunity alone, don't be surprised if in a month or six they're gone on to the next, hot new "faster" business opportunity. This is the most common mistake people make in Network Marketing. It is also the most costly – both personally and professionally!

Contrast the above scenario with the following: You've got a product to sell that has changed your life. Let's say it's a "health" product. A friend told you about it the last time you saw him after you remarked about how great he looked. He offered you some to try. You tried it – and it worked for you, too. It's amazing – you actually feel better and look better than you have in years! You're sleeping better than you can remember – and needing less sleep, at that. And you've even experienced an increase in mental clarity – you remember things you used to forget, and you swear you think faster, even better than back when you were in school more than 20 years ago! Now, what do you suppose it's like for someone listening to you share about your product? "Pretty fantastic" is right! Irresistible, too. Your enthusiasm is genuine – and there's lots of it.

Could you build a successful business sharing and selling a product like that? And six months from now, when you have sponsored 20 people who all felt the same way you do and were out sharing their enthusiasm with others and sponsoring new people every week – do you think you'll have a super successful business on your hands? You bet! And what if, in a month or two, somebody came up to you and said, "Hey, have I got a great money maker for you." Would you drop your business and go running after them? Hardly. And that's the point.

It doesn't have to be a great "health" product, either. Anything people are truly passionate about will do fine. Clean air and water, products that solve any kind of important problem in people's lives, financial services that help people create greater security, etc., all of these and more can make a big difference in people's lives. And that's the key....

## ...Making a Difference

If your product makes a real and lasting contribution to people, you've got the foundation for a tremendously successful Network Marketing business. Add to that the very real chance to share your opportunity with others – what a fantastic life! To quote some ancient and very valuable wisdom:

*If you give a man a fish,*
*you feed him for a day.*
*If you teach him how to fish,*
*you've fed him for a lifetime.*

The retail sale of the product is giving your customer a fish. Sponsoring them into the opportunity is teaching them and helping them feed themselves for a lifetime.

---

The next chapter is titled "Prospecting: Nitty Gritty Tools and Techniques."  To continue our metaphor – now we're going to show you how to be fishers of men and women.

## Chapter 8
# Prospecting: Nitty Gritty Tools and Techniques

*In Network Marketing, prospecting isn't about digging. It's about "sorting" to find the gold.*

# Prospecting: Nitty-Gritty Tools and Techniques

## How to Prospect and Develop a Prospect List

It's not by accident that most people share a very similar visual image for the word *prospecting*. "A miner – forty-niner," with donkey, pick and shovel, out searching for gold... that's what occurs to most people. Some parts of that picture are more true than others. Forget the pick and shovel. All that digging isn't necessary for our kind of prospecting. Panning for gold is more like it. And to be sure – *gold* is what we're after.

An even better analogy to building a successful Network Marketing Organization would be the game of baseball. There are four bases you must reach to score a run. In the Network Marketing business, there are four basic steps to success. The first step – or getting to first base – is "prospecting." This does not mean sponsoring people. Sponsoring is getting to home base. Successful sponsoring occurs when your prospect is using the product, has signed and sent in his or her distributor application, has completed the initial distributor training, made the first retail sale and has sponsored their first distributor. We'll talk more about sponsoring in Chapter 10. Prospecting is the first step. Who are your prospects? Where can you find them? Read on.

## Getting Started

When you first get started, you generally think of a few people right away. But then you begin to wonder, "Who else do I know?" "What's my real potential to build a large organization?" Some people you approach with the opportunity might say, "You know, I really don't know that many people."

We can assure you that your potential *is great*. But before we go into the specifics of just who your prospects are, let's give you two pieces of interesting information that will reveal your true potential as a successful prospector.

First, sociological studies tell us that the average 21 year old knows *800 people*! For many of us, because of travel, telephones, age and experience, the number is far greater than that!

Second, a simple observation of how many people we can reach through the people we already know can be truly astonishing. Everyone in the country, or even the world – if you dare to think that big – knows everyone else through someone else. Repeat: *everyone knows everyone else through someone else*. If there's an exception to this rule – *we don't know it*!

Think about it. Have you ever traveled a thousand or two thousand miles away from home – and met someone who knows someone who you know? It happens all the time. Because of the ease of communications and the mobility of our society today, we easily can reach out to many, many others. How many others? The truth is – *thousands*!!!

By working with those people you know, who can talk with others they know, and so on, your potential is virtually unlimited. This is why a Network Marketing organization, because of its Networking dimension and the compensation structure which fuels it (which is unlike that of any other business), *can* and *will* grow remarkably fast.

Now, you might say, "If my potential is so great and I know so many people, why can't I think of anyone else to contact?" or "I already talked to all the people I thought would be interested – some were and some weren't. Now what do I do?"

First, from what we just covered, it's clear that there are many more people out there to talk to than you have even thought about yet. Second, the biggest mistake that most of us make is that we work out of our heads, using only our thoughts. You can only think one thought at a time, just as you can speak only one word at a time. You think of someone, and then think of someone else, and pretty soon if you don't take positive action on those people, you totally forget about the first person because you're thinking of someone or something else.

We call this "butterfly" thinking, and it's not the best way to start your business. A successful business of any kind generally begins with a plan of action and a clearly defined statement of purpose. Your plan of action will outline the potential of the market, the resources available, and how those resources will be used to achieve your business' goals. This plan provides an overview and reference to keep everyone on track. It's also a standard by which you can measure your productivity and performance, and make adjustments when necessary. However, you don't have to create an extensive business plan to lay a solid foundation for your continuously growing Network Marketing business.

Here's where we get specific about...

## ...How to Build a Successful Network Marketing Organization

First, who do you know, and where are they? It's time to find a pen, if you don't already have one in hand. Let's develop your initial prospect list. We say "initial" because you will be adding to this list constantly as different people come to mind or as you meet new ones. Truth is, we've never met a successful Network Marketer who has ever gotten all the way to the end of his or her prospect list. So many new and great people get added all the time, it's impossible to get to the end.

So, who do you know? First, from your work experience, past and present? Who do you know in your neighborhood? With what people do you do business? Who do you know from church or other religious groups? What about sports and school contacts? Civic clubs and other social organizations? Who has tried to sell you something? From whom did *you* last buy something?

## Prospecting Exercise #1

Let's do an exercise right now that will give you a resource to which you can refer throughout the rest of this book. Get a piece of lined notebook paper, and for exactly three minutes, write down every name you can think of. Don't prejudge them as to whether or not they might be interested. Don't think about them in any way except to write their names down. Find a clock or watch, or have someone time you. And don't worry about spelling at this point, just so long as you can recognize who the names are. Do the exercise now.

This exercise is called "the three-minute head start." With this incredibly simple technique, you now have a head start on all those people who ever went into a Network Marketing program but never knew where to begin.

So, how did you do? Did you get 20 names, 30, 40 or more? If you wrote down *five* names or more, you are ahead of 95 percent of those who have ever been in this business. We mean that literally. Because you've done this simple exercise, you're *way ahead* of most people who ever get started with

Network Marketing. And you've just done what all the successful Network Marketers learn early. Simple, wasn't it? But most people fail in business because they never pay attention to simple *yet essential* details like this. We urge you to get even more ideas about developing a prospect list from the "Prospect List" section in the Appendix of this book.

## Got Your List – Now What?

Now you have something solid to work with – what's next? There are two viewpoints on sharing the business with others. The first is you should talk to everyone you can, as quickly as you can, and a few good people will emerge. This may work if you are a fast talker, or have a good direct mail list and are accomplished in this form of direct-response marketing, or if you have a number of occasions to speak to groups of people or organizations as an expert. But this technique usually doesn't work for the average newcomer to Network Marketing.

The second point of view is you should look for people about whom you know more – and with whom you can be more specific concerning the product, the opportunity and just exactly how you can fill these peoples' needs.

Our experience clearly indicates that the second approach works best for most people. It doesn't waste time and energy, and it improves tremendously your odds of success with those you approach.

## The People-People Business

While from a business perspective, Network Marketing may appear to be a numbers game, in reality, it is a people-people business. It's people who can become dedicated to their purpose and who, through working with others, make Network Marketing work. While anyone *can* do this, there are some people who, because of their current principles and lifestyle, will be more open to the opportunity than others. It is these people you want to approach first. So, before you decide just to whom you're going to talk, let's improve your odds of success – and their odds of success – by doing a brief inventory of your prospect's assets.

## Who Is a Candidate?

In this section, we have listed the different characteristics that will contribute to people's success. The Number One, most important thing to look for is *desire*.

No matter what else people have going for them or how great the opportunity you have to offer, if they don't have a desire to do more, to achieve more in life or to contribute more in some way to themselves or others, you will be wasting your time and theirs.

Now, sometimes people say they don't want anything, but they say this only because they don't believe they can have it. This is something you can help them with, but let's get into that when we are in the section about the specifics of what to say when sharing the opportunity.

Right now, let's look at some of the personal characteristics that are important for success in Network Marketing.

## People Who Are Most Likely to Be Successful

1.   **People who are enthusiastic.** Someone who is naturally excited about life can do an excellent job of talking to others about a product and opportunity they believe in. Enthusiastic people are compulsive "sharers." When they get excited – *look out*! They're perfect.

2.   **People who are spiritually minded.** This is essential for long term success. Without faith in God, people ride a roller coaster of highs and lows through life and can be easily

discouraged. People who know God have the faith to perse-
vere and will work to make others successful. These people
know two important things that guarantee success in Network Marketing: First, "Give and ye shall receive" – and,
"Not my will, but Thy will." In short, they are *giving* people
who have a greater purpose in life than just themselves.
These people are perfect too.

**3.   People who desire more.** Not just more money, but
more from life as well. They may be financially pressured –
people who need a little more income are more open to a
good opportunity. And people with an appetite for a "more
and better" life in general are perfect candidates for the
"Network Marketing Lifestyle."

**4.   People who are speakers and talkers.** These people are
also good candidates, as are those with management experience. They've got a well expanded "comfort zone" and are
more open and able to recognize new opportunities.

**5.   People who already have a flexible work schedule.**
This will allow someone the time to work with others when
they may need it most. They also have a taste of freedom and
flexibility and undoubtedly want more. They're fine candidates.

**6.   People who are visionaries.** These people can see the
end result and will continually be willing to do what it takes
to succeed. They know big dreams are accomplished in small
steps. And they probably have a strong and sincere commitment to making a contribution to others. They're perfect!

**7.   People who have considerable self-esteem.** A person
with a high degree of self-esteem generally will be a leader.
He or she will be believed by others, assuming there are
legitimate reasons for this self-esteem – and there almost
always are. (Self-esteem is very hard to fake!) These people
are excellent choices.

**8.    People who are determined.** Those who are determined will not easily be discouraged by failure. In fact, they may not even recognize the word. These are the kind of people who think everything in life is a learning opportunity. They are right! – and they can't help but be successful.

**9.    People who have previous sales experience.** This person is more likely to know how to talk to people and to help them make a decision. However, they may be *so* good at it that they are difficult or impossible to duplicate. They make many, many sales, but have a difficult time helping others to do the same. Make sure they're able to easily show others how to do what they do. We'll talk more about that later.

**10.  People who have high moral integrity.** This may be the Number One personal asset. This person will be well respected and when they endorse something – everybody knows they can count on it!

**11.  People who have initiative.** This is something you really want to look for. This person will be self-motivated and will not get up at the "crack of noon." Being your own boss and operating your own business takes as much energy, if not more, as does working for someone else. Self-starters do just that – and they tend to continue going strong for a long, long time.

**12.  People who have leadership.** A leader is someone who can inspire others to see *their* own potential – and motivate them to achieve it. Every leader you can sponsor will spawn another group of successful people. And you know what? All great leaders are great followers, too. That's just the way it is.

**13.  People who are hard workers.** There is no substitute for hard work. While Network Marketing may have greater potential than any other business opportunity, the rewards are still in direct proportion to the attention and effort that it's given. Since the rewards can be great, people who are not afraid of hard work can be very successful in this business. In fact, they almost *always* are.

**14. People who are smart workers.** If working *hard* is a prerequisite, learning to work *smart* certainly is a goal to achieve along the way. Smart workers know how to do more with less. Smart doesn't mean lazy, and it doesn't mean getting others to do your work for you. Smart workers are always looking for ways to enable and empower others. They're "smart enough" to know that's the way to have everybody do just a little, and still get a big job done.

**15. People who are survivors.** We may be able to survive in most situations with either a positive or negative viewpoint. However, for people in business for themselves, the optimistic outlook – the one that sees possibilities and turns stumbling blocks into stepping stones – is what you should be looking for. Survivors quickly become "prospers" in Network Marketing.

**16. Sharing, caring people.** Instead of selling, you often hear the word "sharing" in this business. This is because it's closer to "caring." It is caring that makes many people want to let others know the benefits of their products and the opportunity that's available to them. These are also the people who will follow through and help others to succeed. They're perfect, too.

Any one of these characteristics can be the foundation for success. What are some of *your* positive characteristics? What have you learned, developed, or what do you possess that will help you in the building of your business? Take some time now to think about yourself.

Years ago, there was a list in this business that was entitled "The Ideal Prospect." It described all of the traits we just described and more. Many of us who were building organizations back then tried to find someone who fit them all. Of course, this was difficult. Actually, it was impossible. Then we tried telling people that because they didn't have this characteristic or that one, they needed to be in the business to develop it. While people may feel they need the benefits of your product or opportunity, telling them they need a character change is another matter.

By investigating those men and women who had been successful in this business, we found that they all tended simply to use and further develop the strong characteristics they started with. In the process, they naturally became stronger in other areas; however, this is not what motivated them to get started. In other words, instead of looking for a person's weaknesses, look for his or her strengths. Then show them how those strengths and the opportunities you are sharing with them are a perfect marriage. That's what will help them be truly successful.

When people say, "We're broke. We've got nothing to work with. We have nothing to invest," you can always see this is *not true*. Every person has value, characteristics, experience, talents and desires. These are all assets with great economic value – just like money – that people have to invest in their businesses. Some of these assets are worth far more than money. Money gets spent, but personal qualities are more permanent. Qualities like these are also enhanced by applying them to the business and sharing them with others. It's not just your financial freedom that will increase by having your own Network Marketing business – all other freedoms will, too.

Now, let's go back to your prospect list.

## Your First Prospect

To whom on your list do you talk first? Eventually, you may want to talk to them all. There probably is something in your program for everyone. However, you want to get started with those people who are most likely to respond the quickest and in the most positive way. You want to pick those people who have the best chances of early success and work with them first.

While you will never know for sure who these people are, now you can make some highly educated guesses. Again, look for *the desire* in all of your candidates. All desire is good – *burning* desire is best! Have they expressed something to you that they would really love to achieve? Do they have big goals, such as a beautiful home, a brand new car, or to be free from an escalating and disempowering debt? What do they have going for them that we've just covered? Would they be self-starters or leaders? Would they be enthusiastic? Just one of the traits we listed would be a big plus – but what if you found people who had three, or even five or six of them. Review your prospect list and see if you've got a number of "multi-talented" people on it. Begin with them.

## To Get Started, Choose Your Five Best Candidates

Before you ever share an opportunity with people, have a reason to do so that will interest *them*. If you run over and tell them what a great opportunity you have found for yourself, and that they are going to love it because you do, they may simply give you a funny look. More unfortunately, they may give you a closed mind. We humans are self-interested animals. Appeal to that. Don't assume that people want the same things you do or will see an opportunity in the same way that you do. In other words – *first find out what they want.* What is important to them? What are their needs and desires?

Maybe they are looking for an opportunity – maybe not. If they are, it's best to establish that fact up front. Are they tired of their current job, bored, experiencing burn-out? The key is to ask questions. Would he or she be interested in doing something that they could really believe in, be excited about, earn extra income with, and through which they eventually could make more money and enjoy greater freedom than with what they're currently doing?

Also (and this is most important), they should believe in the product and its benefits *before* they are even aware there is a business opportunity – or at the very least, they should consider them together, both at the same time. Then, going into business will be a natural process of sharing the benefits of the product line.

However, taking the step to go into business, or even to look at the possibility or potential of becoming a distributor in Network Marketing, will take some genuine thought and consideration by most people. They may not be happy with their job or would like more freedom and income, but chances are they haven't thought about these ideas lately. How long did it take you to consider such a bold move? That's why you need to ask questions.

There is another prospecting exercise coming up that will help you develop some skill in this area. It is a good role playing exercise that you can do in a training session with other distributors as well. It's designed to work anywhere, anytime and with anyone. You may never find yourself in a situation just like this; however, by practicing this exercise, everything else will be easy.

## Prospecting Exercise #2

Let's assume we don't know each other very well or have never met, which is probably true, and you are going to "prospect" me (for this exercise "we" are "me"):

Casually, you ask me, "What do you do for a living?" The key here is to really listen. Is my response enthusiastic, just matter of fact, or even bored? Don't worry about what you are going to say. Really be interested in me and my response.

I answer, "Well, I develop training programs." If you want to get to know a little more about me, you might ask, "What does that involve?" And, then listen again. Or you could simply ask, "That's interesting, have you ever considered doing something else – something different?"

If I reply, "Yes, I have, I'm kind of tired of this," you can ask, "Well, of all the things you could be doing, what would you like to do most?" I reply, "Well, I'd really like to be a ski instructor in Aspen." Now you have an opening to let me know about a great business opportunity that could eventually allow me to do whatever I want, when and where I want.

Okay, that was easy. But what if I had said, "No, I enjoy what I'm doing and have never thought about doing anything else." Then you could say, "That's great, but have you ever considered doing it in a different way, or on a different scale?" I might answer, "Well, yes, I would like to expand," or, "No, but I would like more free time." You could then say, "Would a substantial increase in your income make it possible to do that?" I would say, "Sure." Then you could invite me to look at a new income opportunity – especially one with a full-time earning potential with part-time hours.

If you'll take the time to role-play this exercise with new distributors in your organization, they will be amazed at how easy it can be to talk to other people and find out all about what they want to achieve. It will also build confidence and be great fun at the same time.

---

Prospecting can be uplifting and a sheer joy – when you take the approach that you are helping others to achieve their goals – as opposed to trying to sell them something. Again, find out what people want. Then show them how to get it. Remember your Million Dollar Attitude – and know for a fact, they want to have one, too.

# Chapter 9
# Effective Presentations as Tools

*Being a successful presenter doesn't take talent or years of training. It just takes knowing how. Here's how.*

# Effective Presentations as Tools

## The Home Meeting Presentation

Well, you know who you want to talk to first, you're well organized and you've got a Million Dollar Attitude – so what do you do now? Now, you give them a presentation. You got to first base by finding out *who they were* and *what they wanted* in the prospecting phase. Getting to second base is accomplished by showing them *how to get what they want*. And you do that in your presentation.

Show and Tell: Tell them the company story. Show them the opportunity that is available for them to build their own business, and tell them how you can help them achieve their personal and professional goals.

Will they all be as enthusiastic as you are and join immediately? Some will – some won't. Some people may simply want the benefits of your products or services. They may have questions about their ability to be successful in the business.

They may wonder who else is doing it, and how are *they* doing? What kind of people are involved? Simply speaking, they want to know if your program *really works* – and if *they* will be able to *work the program*. He or she may think it's a great idea and they know you do, too – but since success involves being able to sponsor others, they want to know if anyone else is able to sponsor. Before they really believe in the possibilities, they want to see proof. Often they will seek one or two others' advice before they fully commit. In most cases, these "others" will have the very same questions. This, of course, can dampen some new peoples' enthusiasm and stop them before they get started. Don't let it. It's all *to be expected*. And as you might expect, we've got a number of things you can do about it.

The number one best answer to all the above is to invite them to a meeting – *first*. Here they can meet "those others," see and catch their enthusiasm and commitment and get a more complete overview of the products and the company's program. Almost all of their questions can be answered immediately. They can see that the program is working because others are involved – excited, enthusiastic and successful!

There may be someone else at the meeting (other than yourself) with whom your guests can identify, because of occupation, background, association or some other common interest. This in itself can help them see more easily that the program can work for them, too.

If there isn't a weekly introductory meeting in your area – begin your own. While the ideal situation is to have a large meeting attended by other distributors and their guests, you can be very effective simply by conducting your own weekly home meeting. Set aside one evening each week to hold this meeting and introduce the program to others. Using the resources and approaches we have discussed up to this point, you can invite your prospects – both retail customers and potential Networkers – as well as the other distributors in your Network and their guests to the meeting.

## Scheduling

These home meetings can be conducted just like any other meeting. Schedule your meetings from 7:30 to 8:30 on a Tuesday or Thursday evening. Ask some of the distributors in your organization or other distributors in the area if they would like to participate. One person could explain the product line; another could present the marketing plan; someone else might be an expert at setting up a product display. If no one else is available, by using your company's support materials (such as brochures) and other sales aids (such as video tapes), you can easily do it yourself. And after one or two meetings, you won't have to do it alone.

Now, let's look at some ideas for an introductory seminar.

## Introductory Seminar Suggestions

Before you can persuade others to buy your product or idea, you need to gain their confidence and help them accept and trust you. The best way to do this is to establish rapport with people by getting acquainted. Be there to greet people at the door. Be friendly and make everyone feel welcome.

## Before the Meeting

Many times people want to go to a meeting and they really intend to go, but when they get home from their job, it's just too tempting to sit down, watch TV and space out while the rest of the world is doing its thing. (By the way, have you ever noticed that people on TV shows never spend their evenings watching TV? Interesting…) If you arrange to pick up your guests or arrange for another friend to do so for you, they'll be there for sure.

Someone once said that "success is not convenient." If you're going to have more success tomorrow than you had today, then you are going to have to *do something different* today than you did yesterday. When you do something different, you are developing a whole new level of your comfort zone. So, you should expect there will be some initial uneasiness. But if you have a strong enough desire to succeed, you will do the uncomfortable thing until it becomes familiar. Honestly, once you start, it won't take long at all. It's waiting to start that feels like an eternity.

If you have given brochures or tapes about the business or the company to your guests beforehand, find out if they have reviewed them.  Make sure any brochure or tape you hand out is of top professional quality, especially when you are showing a tape on the industry or the company with the intention of establishing professionalism and credibility. This is as important – or *more* important – than the message itself. If you are presenting a quality opportunity, then you want everything you do to reflect that high quality. For example, don't take a photocopy of the brochure and say, "Here is what it's all about." Don't give your prospect a tape that has segments missing or has excessive static or tape hiss. In fact, instead of giving people tapes with hand-lettered labels, give them professionally duplicated tapes with printed labels. The tapes are a reflection of the company, the opportunity *and you*. It's only a few dollars per tape. Your professional image is worth this small investment.

People get more out of something the closer they are to it. Second-generation copies of anything present a second-rate image.  They are hazy and fuzzy – and imply that this is a hazy and fuzzy opportunity. If you are really going for it and want to build a successful and first rate, quality organization, go first quality. This point is vital!

One additional point we think is most important – *Dress For Success*. A business suit is still the best. Casual elegance has its place, but for your business – *professionalism* is the key. We know of one instance of a local Distributor Network in Phoenix, Arizona, where it made a huge difference. Phoenix is hot! Not the kind of place where men and women dress in traditional business attire *even for traditional business*. However, this group of people agreed to dress up in their best for every meeting just to see what would happen. Both meeting attendance and new distributor enrollment at the meetings increased dramatically – sales volume increased by 100 per-cent after 30 days! That should be enough motivation to have you give it a try for your meetings.

## Three Things You Want to Accomplish on the Way to the Meeting

1.    Establish or re-establish the purpose, goal or the reason for your prospect to be going to the meeting. Not *your* purpose or goal – *theirs.*

2.    *Prepare them* for the enthusiasm they'll find at the meet-ing.  They may anticipate that it will be boring.  Let them know the people will be excited because they are achieving their goals, making money and having fun doing it. On the way there, try to describe what will take place, so your prospects will know what to expect. If they don't know what to expect, or if they expect something and it's different, they may become turned off. Help them become comfortable with what is going to be happening – or, you may lose them because they did not see or hear what they expected. Most people behave in a very conservative manner when they are among strangers. Prepare your guests for the enthusiastic and exciting atmosphere.

A friend of ours, Dave, was invited by his friend, Duane, to attend a Network Marketing meeting.  Duane didn't prepare Dave for what he would see and hear there. After the meeting, Dave announced that he was completely turned off, and described the atmosphere as being like "a carnival sideshow or a religious tent-revival meeting." Dave's re-sponse could easily have been avoided if Duane made sure to prepare him for what would happen there.

3.    *Sell them* on the speakers. Introductions for a speaker are intended to establish authority as to why he or she is quali-fied to speak on the subject. Without that kind of introduc-tion, audience members will spend too much time checking

each person out in their minds. Do they know what they're talking about? Where are they coming from? What is their experience? Pre-sell your guests on your speakers' credibility. You want them to have positive expectations about what each person is going to say and how they are going to say it. Like sharing anything else, don't "make a technical case" for the speaker – or for the meeting, for that matter. Just share your own experience and enthusiasm about the speakers. That works best.

## Set Them Up for Success

A presentation really begins with your pre-meeting conduct. Arrive at least 30 minutes earlier than the scheduled time. Everything that takes place before the meeting will color the newcomer's perception of the business opportunity. Design your pre-meeting conduct and the presentation itself, so that it has the maximum effect of helping people understand the opportunity. When people witness a presentation, they have only an hour to see and understand a success story that has taken years to develop. For any other profession we might choose as a career, we might not be able to even define it in that short period of time. Yet, here the newcomer is, looking at an entire and fairly complex Network Marketing career opportunity. Therefore, it's very important that you present the opportunity in as effective and engaging a manner as possible.

This begins with your pre-meeting conduct. When you bring your guests to the meeting, do you tell them to sit down and behave, because it will start pretty soon? *That* would make them feel very uncomfortable. The important thing is for guests to be relaxed and to be made to feel a part of what's going on. Develop a friendly rapport with them before the meeting starts. Get to know them better by asking questions and listening intently to their answers.

When you meet someone, greet them and call them by their first name. Have everyone wear name tags, so that you can remember their names when you introduce them to others. By the way, wear the name tag on your right lapel, not your left, so that when you shake hands with people, it is more natural to see their name tags easily.

Make good eye contact without staring them down.

Shake hands in a straight-forward manner, without being dominant or passive. The way people shake your hand can indicate their personality traits. For example, if they roll their hand on top of yours, they want to dominate, they like to be in control. If they exhibit dominance or controlling behavior in the handshake, talk to them about leadership. Here is a chance to be a leader, to be in control.  If they roll their hand under yours, that's more passive; that person wants someone to tell them what to do. If they shake hands passively, talk to them about an opportunity that provides leadership for them to follow and stress the fact that in Network Marketing, you don't have to "do it all by yourself."

Shake hands with a women the same way you shake hands with a man – a nice firm handshake, unless she does not offer her hand.

So, what you are going to do is bring your guests in and introduce them to others, just as others will introduce their guests to you. Develop a family atmosphere. Ask questions that will help you understand their interests and give you some indication of how compatible they may be with the business.

**"What kind of work do you do now?"** (The answer will tell you their level of income and the hours they work. It will also let you know how much they like or are committed to their work.)

**"Does your spouse work?"** (The answer to this question will let you know if one of them is a potential full-time candidate for the program.)

**"How long have you lived in the area?"** (The answer will let you know how established they are in the community, and how easy it could be for them to get started in the business.)

All of these questions will make guests feel comfortable and help you to better understand each person as an individual.

In order for the presentation to be effective, it has to be built on a purpose, a reason for them to be there. Remember this. We often are so excited about the opportunity that we want to tell people all the wonderful things about it, but we forget to relate it to something that they can identify with – some way that it can *directly benefit them.*

Everything you do before the meeting and during the meeting is a reflection on the opportunity you are presenting.

The introduction to the meeting is vital. You need to get everyone's favorable attention and win their confidence. You can get attention by screaming, shouting or calling their attention to something negative such as bad weather conditions or a terrible situation you saw on TV. This is not "favorable attention." You get favorable attention by establishing some purpose or need that can be fulfilled by really listening to, and being fully present at, this meeting. Remember that some of them may have felt coerced into coming to the meeting, or they may have come "against their better judgment," or could not find a graceful way to get out of attending. They may have made up their minds that they'll come to the meeting but say "no," regardless of how wonderful the opportunity turns out to be. You need to neutralize these attitudes right up front. Think about their concerns.

## The Meeting Agenda

Whatever you start with should be something that really gets their attention. You could begin by telling them that tonight, you're going to show them how to solve the most common problem facing people today – or – you could tell them that there is a fantastic opportunity that could change their lives forever, etc. Here are a couple of examples of things to say (and notice how effective it is to open with a question):

- "How many of you would enjoy more prosperity in your lives *starting right now?*"

- "What if the thing you wanted to achieve most in your life was actually on its way to you right now – wouldn't that be great?

Let your initial question hang just a little. Most of the time, they'll answer you as a group. If not, search out agreement from a number of people through making eye contact and even asking them directly, "Mark, would you enjoy being more prosperous?"

Now, take a moment to establish credibility about Network Marketing as a viable, dynamic, even extraordinary business. *This is very important!* If you don't make the case for Network Marketing right up-front, you risk having all you say fall on deaf ears. Many people have questions, real or imagined, about our business. There's a lot of good information about Network Marketing you can use in Chapter One. Don't make this long-winded and don't come off as defensive. Just state the powerful track record and extraordinary growth possibilities – drop a couple of names and move on.

After that, state the facts simply about your company and its management. Tell the story. Point out its accomplishments. What's the company's vision? What is its purpose? How has it helped distributors – like you, for instance – achieve their goals? Explain how this opportunity can provide the means to achieve their goals – to turn their dreams into reality.

Why have the explanation of the company *before* the product or opportunity? Because people always want to know who's behind the the products and the plan. Many times in Network Marketing, you'll get someone interested in a company based on its dynamic leadership, or the empowering and far reaching corporate vision, so the company should actually come first. Also, if people have doubts about the company, whatever is said or even personally experienced – about the products or the business opportunity – will stand against a background of doubt until the company itself is understood and it's people, management, motives and track record are held in good regard.

After you lay the foundation so they understand what the company is about, you should present the product line. Showing the products is a must. Get them into their hands if you can. If it's something that has a great taste, look, smell, etc., let them experience it right then and there. Nothing beats "a talk and a taste." Explain, or even better, demonstrate, the benefits of the products or service if you can. Have others share their personal experiences of how they have benefited from using the product. This last point is crucial. It's one of the most important parts of every meeting.

Next, present the marketing plan. Be enthusiastic about it. Remember always to include the "you" benefits – what it has to offer *them*. The purpose of the presentation is to show them how to get what they want to achieve. For most people, achievement will involve earning additional income. So, when you relate the marketing opportunity, you should show them, as specifically as possible, how it will work for them. If there is someone in your group who is good with numbers, have him or her do this part. If not, and you' re not sure just how to do it, use the illustration in your company brochures or distributor's manual to explain how the plan works. Write the figures on a chalk board or with magic marker on a flip chart just as they are illustrated in the company's material.

If there are other distributors at the meeting who have helped you organize or put it on, acknowledge them and thank them publicly.  Also congratulate any other distributors at the meeting on their recent accomplishments, especially the achievement levels they have reached in the company. And make a point of congratulating new people on their decision to join. This is obviously great for them, and it also helps your guests see how much they'll be appreciated as well. Make everybody feel good about themselves and what they've done.

Wrap up the meeting with a brief summary of what's been covered – ending with what's being offered. If you can tell an inspiring story that will motivate people, do it here. Relate how the product or opportunity has helped you or another person you know about, preferably in a unique, even extraordinary way. Challenge everyone to action, including the distributors themselves. Many times the distributors come to the meeting to recharge their energy and renew their enthusiasm for the business opportunity. Give them what they came for.

## Closing Exercise

You can close by saying: "Turn to the person who brought you here, and share with them what you think is available for you with this product and opportunity."

Then say, "If you can see some real value here for you with these great products and this opportunity, ask your partner, 'What do I need to do to get started in this business?' Take a moment and do that now." Thank them for coming – wish them your best and say good night.

After the formal part of the meeting is over, keep yourself available for everybody. People will tend to break up into smaller, informal groups, so they can get their questions answered and have an opportunity to enroll as a new distributor. Give them an opportunity to look over the products. Answer specific questions, but remember to focus on personal experience and benefits – not technical details. Keep it personal by asking questions of them that cause them to consider what's in it for them. This is a great time to serve some simple refreshments, which helps people relax and encourages them to stick around and speak personally with others.

## A Few Key Points for Your Meetings:

• **Hold meetings on a regularly scheduled basis.** The "same time – same place" system allows people to count on attending the meeting and making it part of their business routine – and they don't have to remember where and when it's going to be. These meetings will help your new people a great deal. It gives them a place to bring their prospective distributors where they can count on having all the experience they don't have yet and the support they need to succeed.

• **Solicit help and support from other distributors in your organization or in the area.** It's especially important to have your sponsor and his or her sponsor there if at all possible. Success breeds success. And these successful Networkers are an inspiration to new people, and very persuasive as well. This point is especially helpful when you're just starting out, because you can't prove how successful you are yet – but they can! The more everyone works together, the greater the potential will be for everyone's personal and professional success. Remember, this _is_ Networking – and it's very, very powerful stuff.

• **Keep the meetings as objective as possible.** This isn't to say don't share your subjective experience and enthusiasm. The point is, these meetings are not training sessions for distributors per se. Keep it focused on the introduction to the products and the plan. That's the purpose. Leave discussions of problems and "how to do the business" for training meetings.

• **Keep your meeting on a professional level.** If home meetings are the only meetings available, be aware (or beware) of the tendency they naturally have to become social affairs or gossip sessions, which, of course, you don't want. Introductory meetings in the home, with or without other area meetings, can potentially help you to develop a great initial group of distributors. Just be sure to keep the home meetings objective and positive. When you let people know clearly in advance what the meeting is for and how it will be conducted, this won't be any problem.

• **Stick to the announced time schedule!** Let everyone involved know precisely when the meeting starts and when it will be over. Start on time, no matter who's there. And be sure to dismiss the meeting at the time agreed upon. If the guest you brought wants to stay a little later, that's fine – stick around. Being on time is a simple way to make and keep commitments. It shows respect for yourself and others, and that you are organized and professional.

One important point. We don't want to discourage anybody, but there may be a time, especially in the beginning, when so few people show up that you think about calling the meeting off. *Don't do it*! Here's a story a friend told us that illustrates this point beautifully:

Robert had planned to give the first meeting of his new Network Marketing career. Five people had agreed to come – four prospects and one "upline" distributor, and one of the prospects was the guest of another prospect. Confirmation calls had been made the evening before and the meeting was all set. Everything was well planned and well rehearsed. Robert was *ready*. However, he did not count on a cold, gray Tuesday at the end of a New England March turning into *a cloudless blue sky and 78° humdinger!* It was the most beautiful day of the year and everybody was out in shorts and tee-shirts saying *"good-bye"* to winter. Nobody came.

Robert had asked everybody to come at 7:00, so they could all get to know each other. The meeting was set to begin at 7:30. At the appointed time, he went into the living room, took all the pillows off the couch and propped them up on the meeting chairs he had arranged for the participants. Robert proceeded to make his complete presentation – *to the assembled pillows!* To the best of his and our knowledge, it is the first time in the history of Network Marketing that four pillows signed up to become distributors all in the same night!

To this day, Robert says that night his life changed and took on a whole new dimension. He said he learned more about Network Marketing, what kind of commitment it took to succeed in this business – and about himself – than at any other time in his life. Today, Robert is a very successful, long-term Network Marketing distributor. He started his career by making his first presentation to five pillows!

The point is, *no matter what*, do the meeting as planned. You never know what will happen. And you never know what will come of it. Even a meeting where nobody came changed Robert's life forever. Do the meeting *no matter what*.

## Setting Up the Meeting Room

As your group grows, it will be necessary to look for a meeting room that will accommodate larger groups of people. If there is not another meeting going on in a facility in which you can participate, then you should talk to other distributors and work together to organize one.

It's good for everyone to have a large, common meeting where you can take strong prospective distributors. There, they can see and experience more of what's going on in the area and with the company. Also, more people can share the responsibility of putting on the program.

When you are ready to move your meetings into a regular meeting room facility, be sure to do your homework first:

•   Check out prospective locations to see if they are conducive to doing business. If someone says he can come up with a meeting room for very little money, or next to nothing, it may be worth just that. On the other hand, sometimes you can find a great room in a church, school or library that will work perfectly.

The physical atmosphere and logistics of a meeting say as much about the opportunity as the speaker.

## Ideal Conditions

The Appendix of this book includes a meeting room diagram and a list of ideal conditions to look for when selecting your room site.  It's not always possible to find all of these conditions, but try your best to arrange for the room to have as much of the following as possible:

• A 6-12 inch high stage or platform riser
• A large, clean chalk board with dustless chalk and an eraser – *and/or* – Two flip charts with easel pads
• A lectern or podium
• A national flag
• A company banner
• A microphone with a 30 foot cord
• Elevated product displays to show off the product line
• Theater style seating with a center aisle
• An entry door at the rear of the room
• A ceiling height of at least 10 feet

- Fluorescent lighting
- Carpet on the floor rather than tile or wood
- No mirrors or windows
- Comfortable chairs
- Light, neutral colors rather than dark ones

You may never find all of these features in one room, but together they create a better atmosphere than, for example, having a doorway come in from the front of the room where you are speaking, or having mirrors along the wall that distract people during your presentation.

You want carpeting so that the room is quieter. You want a high ceiling. You want good lighting – as natural as possible. If it is a dark room, what does that say about the opportunity? That it's a *dim* opportunity.

Don't try to save money by getting a small chalk board. A little board says: "little opportunity." It is a subconscious communication that goes on: big board = big opportunity. If you're using flip charts, here's a great tip: Using magic markers, put a frame on each page. Simply draw a line using the fat edge of the marker about one to two inches in from the edge of the paper, completely around the perimeter of the large page. Do this for every page – those that already have writing and charts on them, and the blank pages you'll be writing on during the presentation as well. This little trick adds so much to the professionalism of your presentation, you'll have to see it in action to believe it. Remember, everything that goes on in this room reflects the quality of the opportunity.

The geographical location of the meeting room is *very* important. You don't want to present a great opportunity in a questionable part of town. Will people go there for a meeting? Maybe, but most likely not. You want a nice area with plenty of well-lit parking. All these things reflect upon your opportunity.

Once you find a room that meets as many of these guidelines as possible, you should do these things before the meeting:

- Set up a registration table outside of the meeting room.
- Set up only 75 percent of the chairs and stack the rest at the back of the room.
- Arrange for a water table in the back of the room.
- Arrive one hour early and make sure the room temperature is set at 65 degrees.

If you are conducting a home meeting, that's a whole different story. You have something there that you don't have in a formal meeting room. You have more comfort and more acceptance on the part of participants. If you meet in a home, remember – don't make it a social hour. Be sociable, but stay objective. Make sure you have someone baby-sit small children so that they do not become a distraction. Treating the family to dinner and a movie on the night of your meeting is the best thing of all.

Whether you choose to set up and support a large meeting or have a smaller session in your home, be cordial, but keep the meeting on a professional level and stick to the business at hand. Remember, it *is* a business – *your business.* And it is a profession, and like any other, if you treat it that way, it will compensate you as a professional.

## Area Meetings

Let's take a closer look at an area meeting. An area meeting will provide you with an additional prospecting tool. For example, you may talk to someone about the business whom you would feel more comfortable taking to one of these meetings, rather than inviting them to a private home. Perhaps you have given a brochure to someone who is accustomed to a business atmosphere. This is someone who you may want to pick up and take to a meeting where they might meet others with similar interests who are already in the program.

This business is a people-people business – regardless of the people's background. You need to get to know all your prospective customers and distributors, develop a relationship with them, pay special attention to what it is they want to achieve and make sure they see how *you* will *help them achieve it.*

The most effective way to do this is to spend exclusive time with your prospective distributor when he or she is introduced to the program. Ideally, you should arrange to pick up your guest and take him or her to the meeting. This way you will be sure that you have a guest who already feels he or she is important to you and supported by you – *even before they sign up.*

## Summary

Let's take another look at the meeting format and explore what you can do to ensure its success.

Whether you help to organize the meeting, conduct it or simply use it to introduce prospective distributors, you can contribute to the overall success of the program. While the basic format will follow the same outline that we talked about for a home meeting, the general atmosphere, your conduct and that of everyone else present is very important to the meeting's success.

The purpose of the presentation is to help the guests understand the benefits of the product and the program and to take positive action – i.e., *to sign up as a distributor in your Network.* It is important to remember that the environment is an image and reflection of the company, the opportunity and you. The presentation should:

1.   **Reflect prosperity and success** and be alive with enthusiasm. Leave any negative feelings or attitudes – as well as people – at home.

2.   **Keep the meeting room free of distractions.** We're not just talking about a pillar in the middle of the room. Scenic views through an open door can be just as distracting. At a Network Marketing meeting held in a Los Angeles, California, resort hotel, a gap in a room partition revealed attractive male and female models readying themselves to walk out in front of an audience in the next room. Needless to say, few Network Marketers and their prospects heard what the speaker had to say. It is wise to check what will be next door to your meeting room on your meeting date. Holding your meeting next to a wedding reception doesn't work at all!

3.   **Be professional and efficient,** so that things go step-by-step as planned. Make sure the meeting room atmosphere appears natural, effortless and efficient. In order for you to do that, work hard, be aware and be prepared. Make certain everything is set up properly – that the meeting flows, instead of jerks along. That's why you need to arrive early and check everything in advance. Assume that nothing will work – because at least one thing *won't!* Find out which one doesn't work early, and adjust it.

4.   **Make the meeting room atmosphere conducive to making natural and positive decisions.** While you want to be well prepared, be sure you are "real." Don't present yourself as something you're not. Simply let your sincerity and enthusiasm show for the products and business you're sharing with your guests.

Prepare a check sheet of everything you need to take to the meeting. Arrive in plenty of time to set it up. It might be a good idea to carry everything you need in the trunk of your car, so you will always be prepared.

## Three Things that Move Most People to Action

- **Enthusiasm** – This comes from expecting something good.
- **Recognition** – Remember the names of new distributors as well as top producers.
- **Acceptance** – Develop good eye contact and a firm hand-shake.

During the meeting, it's very important to check your body language. For example, let's say you bring a guest to the meeting tonight to see the business for the first time. Now, you've been to lots of meetings, and to this particular meeting at least 20 times. So, you think you know everything that is going to happen and you're also a bit tired. You sort of slouch, instead of sit up straight, and move around a lot to get as comfortable as possible. Your body actions tell your guest a story: "I have seen this before and boy is it boring." You're sending a clear message that is not consistent with what you told them about the meeting. You told them there was a great opportunity here, but now, your body says, "There's nothing to get excited about." As a result, your guest will be confused and may have trouble figuring out which impression is true. Chances are, they'll choose the last one, because that's what's true for them *right now*!

Realize that if you have a meeting every week and the speaker has found a way that best tells the story, then he or she is going to say basically the same thing each time. Also, a speaker's effectiveness can depend a great deal on your enthusiastic support. If we tell our guests to listen carefully while we slouch in our chairs, click our ballpoint pens, file our nails, catch up our appointment books, take short naps or otherwise indicate our boredom and disinterest, we are not supporting the speakers nor the purpose of the meeting. An easy way to do this, is for you to take notes. That supports the speaker *and* your guest as well.

Remember, it is the first time your guest has seen this presentation. Act as though it's the first time you have seen it, because it *is* the first time you have seen it in this exact situation or setting. If you really listen, you will always find a new way to apply or use the material. If necessary, be a good actor. Actors in long-running plays or Broadway hits play the same role night after night, sometimes for years. Because they are professionals, they know it's the first time members of the audience have seen their performance. They accept this as their professional responsibility and make it seem new, and fresh and wonderful each and every time.

So again, watch your body language. It will affect the way you listen. You don't need to sit on the edge of your chair, but at least sit up and pay attention. Your guest will most likely mirror your body language. Keep your attention on the speakers. Let them tell the story and give them your complete support.

Many of you will have an opportunity to conduct meetings yourself for the first time. You will also do presentations and some trainings as well. You'll find that the support given to the speaker will be reflected to the guests who are there. The speaker generally reflects the people who they are with. Support that person as best you can. If you support them, they will support you – and everyone wins.

---

In conclusion, your presentation meeting's atmosphere should appear effortless and efficient. Keep the meeting simple and believable – that's the essence of powerful presentations. Have your opening and closing mastered to the point that you appear natural and spontaneous. This will allow everyone to act and respond in the best and most positive way. And what's more, it will enable you to get the results you want.

# Chapter 10
# Sponsoring Your Prospect

*"Should I or shouldn't I?" It's
always a choice. Here's what you
need to do to make the "right choice."*

# Sponsoring Your Prospect

If this was a book on conventional sales techniques, this chapter would be titled "Closing Your Prospect." However, "closing" implies simply "the end" of the process – and that's *not* what we want to tell you about.

No matter what the outcome of your phone call, meeting or presentation – your goal is to always "keep the door open." Remember, Network Marketing is a business of timing. If your prospect doesn't *buy or sign up today*, that's not the end of it. The simple truth is, the timing just wasn't right for them – *YET*. Everything changes. Perhaps a week or a month from now things will be different. Your prospect may develop new circumstances in his or her life that make your product more attractive and appealing. Undoubtedly, your presentation will change and become better and better. Their job or income situation might have taken a dramatic turn which makes them much more open to your opportunity. And always, your increasing success will be a more and more powerful motivational factor.

Another point that's really important to draw here is about the word "complete." To be complete is to lack nothing, to have all the elements. It comes from the Latin *complere*: to fill up or fulfill. Being complete with a prospect is a positive goal that you can *always* achieve – no matter how your prospect responds. If your success is based outside of yourself, on how they respond, you will always be *reacting*, or at the mercy of their decisions. That's not very empowering for you, and it's not very creative, either. If you "have all the elements," even if your prospect says, "No," you are a success! So, aim for completing with your prospect and don't worry about whether they say yes or no. With this approach, you'll quickly get a higher and higher percentage of yeses than you ever imagined possible.

Being "complete" with your prospect is required before you can successfully sponsor them.

## The Third Step in Building a Successful Organization

Remember our baseball analogy? Making it to first base was prospecting. During the initial prospecting process, you found out *what your prospects wanted*. Reaching second base, in the presentation, you showed them *how to get it*. In reaching completion with your prospect, you round third base and you're heading for home – successfully sponsoring them into the business.

Sponsoring really is a two phase process. We'll talk now about the first phase – where you find out whether or not your prospective distributor believes that he or she can enjoy the benefits of your product and be successful in this business. In the next chapter on Following Through, we'll complete the sponsoring process.

While some prospects may see other distributors at the meeting who believe in the program and who have reached various levels of achievement, the telling factor is whether or not your prospects believe *they can do it, too*. Initial sponsoring techniques all should revolve around helping your guests see how they can be successful, either through your support, through the support of others, through company training programs, etc. When you do your job by being complete with your prospects, you've done your best to bring them to a point of making an informed choice.

There is a lot of material written about traditional "closing" techniques. It is a course in itself, and also a lifetime pursuit to learn all the subtle ways to get people to do what you want. However, let us share with you an important point before we go into our "Completing Exercises."

People make decisions emotionally. Whether or not they follow through will be based on logic and on whether or not they know *how* to follow through. *Never manipulate someone into this business.* Why? Simply because any relationship based on manipulation will *fail* sooner or later! It should be a soft sell, a natural process based on logic and truth. The motivation for people to take initial action will generally have to be there for them to take the next step. In short, they have to be open to it – *they have to want to do it.* Although you may have to create an opening for them, you accomplish this by effectively communicating the benefits of the product and opportunity – and then asking them to make a choice.

If you push people into this business by tricking or forcing them, against their nature, they will respond emotionally and negatively. If they really don't believe they can do it, what are you going to have to do to get them to continue in the business – or even to go to the next meeting? You constantly will have to manipulate them – you'll have to push and pull them to do everything. And believe us, they'll "hate" you for it.

Remember, you are trying to build an organization of independent, self-reliant business people. You want them to be as genuinely motivated as possible. If people aren't motivated to come into the business, do you really want them in your organization? Of course not. It's got to be their idea. Without that idea being *theirs*, you will only be able to work with a couple of people at most, because you will be out hustling and "baby-sitting" all the time. That's not the way to grow a business. What you want is to get your new distributors started in the program and work with them until it really catches on in their lives. Eventually, for these new distributors and for yourself to grow and prosper, they need to do what you do – *on their own*.

## Inform, Involve and Inspire

To be complete with your prospect, to give them the opportunity to make a choice to say "yes" or "no," you'll have to accomplish each of the following:

**Inform:** This means to give them information, but even more, it means to give them the *right* information. That means the benefits. Expertly conveying all the features and technical aspects of a product or plan never got anybody to choose to become involved. In fact, many people get caught up in all the details just to avoid having to make a choice! When you share the benefits through your personal testimony (and that of others) you are giving people the information they really want. And the result is that they become personally involved.

**Involve:** All the fantastic benefits in the world won't make people make a positive choice if they don't see themselves involved. People can "see" your information – what you're saying – in their minds. Your goal is to have them *feel* it as well. Your prospect must *see and feel how* they will benefit from using the products, they need to *see and feel how* they will be able to make the business opportunity work. The best way to involve someone is to paint a picture and put them into it. You do this by asking questions, finding out what they want, and then showing them how the products and the opportunity you're offering will do it for them. When you do that, you're past third base – headed for home plate. These people are ready to be inspired.

**Inspire**: If *inform* is to give somebody the "form" of it, *inspire* is to give them the *spirit*. When you inspire your prospects about your product and opportunity – sponsoring them into the business is inevitable. What's more, after they sign up, they will hit the ground running and probably never stop!

Inspiring people isn't reserved only for super-stars or expert motivational speakers. In fact, the most inspirational thing for most people is an ordinary person doing something extraordinary. Look back over the incredible benefits of your product, the personally and professionally empowering concept of Network Marketing, the remarkable opportunity for satisfaction and fulfillment, personal and financial freedom and the ability to live a lifestyle of genuine success and abundance that you're offering your prospects. Meeting you could be the thing that will change their lives forever. Now, *that* is inspirational!

*You* have all it takes to inform, involve and inspire people. With a little practice and making sure you're complete with each one of them – you'll be able to do it every time.

## Make Sure They Truly Understand

After the introductory program, how are you going to be complete with your prospects?

First, you must make sure they clearly understand the opportunity. Many of us have been in a program for six months and still didn't understand the compensation plan. Most of us only assume the program will work and then decide *on faith* to go for it, but we have difficulty explaining it to our prospects. In that situation, we are not being as effective as we could be and we can't be complete with people. In the end, we'll *lose* more people than we *find*.

Ask them if they see how the program will help them obtain what they want out of life. Be specific. If you know what they want, help them out by referring to it. For example:

"Robert, do you see how becoming involved in this program can put you into that new car that you want?" or "...pay for your daughter's college education?" or "...get you out of debt?"

"You do. That's great. Now, let's get started. Here's what *we* have to do next."

If they reply, "No, I don't quite see it," that's incomplete. Ask them what it was they think they didn't understand fully. Help them or find someone who can explain it to them if you aren't able to do so.

Completing is based upon fully meeting people's needs. All their needs. In order to meet those needs, you must find out what they are and what truly motivates and inspires people. Let's put down a few hints about what most people want most.

- Peace of mind
- Freedom
- Feelings of accomplishment
- Recognition
- Financial independence
- Material possessions
- A business of their own
- Tax advantages
- Security
- Achievement
- Public acceptance
- Self-acceptance
- Health
- More income
- Convenience
- Good relationships
- To have a great time

Acceptance really motivates and inspires people. If you have been in this business for a while, you have grown and developed personally and professionally. You have become a part of an organizational family. Often, we get more acceptance from the organization than we do from many of our own blood relatives. People can see that. This is a business of people working together so that we all can achieve our goals, both collectively and individually.

Not only are people inspired by the things they truly want – they also are motivated to avoid the loss of something they already have. Fear of loss is a strong motivator.  People are afraid of losing control of their freedom, their circumstances or of life itself.

Some common fears are:

- Fear of embarrassment
- Fear of taking undue risks
- Fear of criticism
- Fear of pain-both mental and physical – and  the pain of change
- Fear of failure
- Fear of loss

It's best to emphasize positive motivators, but you need to be aware of the negative ones, too, and of what people fear. Leaving these fears in place keeps you incomplete with your prospect. So sometimes, you will need to deal with the fears people have, but you also want to be very careful to avoid any words or phrases which invoke their negative or doubtful emotions.

Here are some examples of positive phrases you can use to help convince them of the value of this business opportunity:

**"Isn't this a really great opportunity?"**

**"Do you see how becoming a distributor could really change your life?"**

**"Don't you agree that the best parts of this program are the benefits of the products?"**

**"Haven't they done an incredible job on working out the compensation plan?"**

Did you notice that each statement was designed to get them to agree on one simple issue? Use these terms with positive statements. And always talk in terms of benefits.

Sprinkle some of these "agreement" phrases throughout your presentation:

**"...Isn't that right?"**

**"Aren't they....?"**

**"Didn't it....?"**

**"Doesn't it....?"**

**"Won't you....?"**

**"Wouldn't you....?"**

In your notebook, reserve a space to list minor agreements of a positive nature. Write down any you can think of, learn them word for word and use them in your presentations.

Now, we also want to give you a list of words and phrases that you're better off avoiding, so that people won't become angry or feel hostile or manipulated. These phrases can be interpreted as "put-downs" and can trigger a negative psychological reaction, even though they appear perfectly logical on the surface.

Avoid these phrases:

**"Maybe you never thought of this before, but...."**

**"You probably don't know this, but...."**

**"I am going to prove to you...."**

**"I know better than you...."**

"I have had more experience than you...."

"When you have lived as long as I have...."

"Don't ask me why, just do what I tell you...."

"I'm only telling you this for your own good...."

"What you're trying to say is...."

"Here's what I want you to do...."

"I hope you're not going to be mad at me, but...."

"When I was your age...."

It is far better to use positive phrases that help encourage people's pride, give them a feeling of importance, and empower their cooperation.

Try instead to use phrases like:

"What do you think of this...?"

"Have you ever tried this...?"

"Let's try to figure out what caused this problem...."

"Did you ever consider that...?"

"I wonder what the best solution would be for...?"

"Try looking at it this way...."

Say "seldom" instead of "never."

Say "usually" instead of "always."

You "must" *always, never* say "must"!

Don't make people feel inferior. Nourish their self-esteem. Don't rob them of their right to make a decision. Give them a choice whenever you can. Being too direct is often offensive. It is more tactful to be subtle or to persuade by suggestion. It should always appear that the wise choice they made was of their own free will.

After you show people how the program will help them get what they want, emphasize *your* support *for them*. Let them know you are going to help them get their business going. Make them aware of their support group of up-line sponsors. Tell them all about the company training programs and support material. Listen to what they have to say and respond directly to it.

Find out what motivates the other person and go for that. See things from their viewpoint. Find out what they want, show them how to get it and then motivate them to take action. Have some trust in them – and in yourself and your opportunity. If your presentation is *complete* – they'll make the right choice. And that's to be sponsored by you into the business.

Once you have accomplished this, you have crossed third base and are rounding the corner towards home. Successful sponsoring doesn't end with your prospect sending in his or her distributor application. As we said in the beginning of Chapter Eight, true sponsoring is accomplished only when your prospect has attended the new distributor training, shared and sold the products retail and sponsored their first person into the business. In truth, sponsoring is a long-term commitment you make with each one of the people in your Network Marketing Organization. We'll explain that next.

# Chapter 11
# Follow Through

*In Network Marketing, as in any endeavor, Follow Through is what gives you power for success.*

# Follow Through

The fourth step in building a successful Network Marketing organization is to follow through with your new distributors until they, too, become successful. It's follow through that gets you to home base, scoring more and more runs for your team. You can enroll hundreds of people into this business, but without following through with them, you're really kidding yourself about being serious and building an organization. Follow Through = Sponsoring.

A tennis player will achieve very little if he or she stops the racquet's forward motion the moment the ball is hit. The ball will have little velocity and no possibility of top spin or backspin. In short, if it does manage to get over the net, it does so weakly and without power. Think of a golfer's swing, throwing a football, hitting a baseball – any action in which the graceful arc of follow through is a fundamental part of mastering the game's technique.

A Network Marketer who does his or her prospecting perfectly, makes a great initial presentation and brings the prospect to an informed, involved and inspired "Yes," *yet doesn't follow through* with responsibility, training and support, has very little hope of creating a successful relationship – much less a growing, successful Network Organization. In sports as in business – in fact, in every aspect of your life – follow through is required for success.

Let us share this example with you that shows just how important follow through is.

A gentleman who had become very successful in this business was conducting a seminar several years ago in Phoenix, Arizona. He had been with his company for 15 years. He was so financially successful that he had just ordered a $1.8 million Mitsubishi jet aircraft for his own private use. He had tens of thousands of people in his organization. When asked for the key to his success, he said, "In 15 years, I have directly sponsored only 100 people, maybe less."

That meant he signed up and kept six or seven key people a year, right? How could he possibly have been so successful with such small numbers? What he did was to master the art of forming mutually supportive, enduring relationships.

Now, we are not telling you that you need to sponsor only two or three people. You may have to work with 50 to get five who are really serious. But whomever you sponsor into the business, be sure that you take the time to work with them as much as necessary to get them started – and to follow through on the commitment you made to them in getting them into the business in the first place.

You told them: "I am here to help you, and I will support you in all your efforts."

If you are going to sponsor a lot of people directly, be sure the systems and the programs are available to help you help them to achieve what they want. Your job is to provide them with all they need in this business to take off and run with it. The key here is the word *sponsor*.

## Recruiting versus Sponsoring

In Network Marketing, some people *recruit* and others *sponsor*. What's the difference? They're both about success-fully bringing more people into your group – right? Yes, but they are really very different words.

To *sponsor* is to "vouch for, or be responsible for a person or thing." A *sponsor* is, "a person who makes a pledge on behalf of another." *Sponsor* comes from the Latin, *spondere*, meaning, "a solemn promise; one who gives surety." One dictionary goes so far as to suggest that *to sponsor* "is to assume accountability for another's spiritual growth and development" (which, with the addition of providing financial security, is the accepted definition of being appointed a child's Godmother or Godfather). The same root is found in the word *responsible*. And there's an interesting connection with the word *spontaneous*, which means, "by nature or natural impulse."

To *recruit* is "to raise by enlistment, such as enlisting in the armed forces." Recruit comes from the French, *recrue*. Jean Baptiste Racine, the French playwright (1639 - '99), encountered the word *recrue* when it first appeared in gazettes in Holland and deemed it "barbarous." *Recruit* seems forever connected with the military. If you look to the Latin, *recruit* comes from two words; *re*, "again," and *crescere*, "to grow."

It's up to you whether you choose to *sponsor* or *recruit*. At face value, the personalities of the words seem pretty much the same. You can *sponsor* and vouch for someone – be responsible for them and "give them surety." And you can *recruit*, enlist them and "again grow" your organization. It's the essence or soul of each of these words that seems to distinguish them from one another.

Which would you rather be – *recruited* or *sponsored*? Clearly, to *sponsor* people requires taking *responsibility* for them. By definition, it requires the making and keeping of a "solemn" promise. As we've seen, it's a "pledge" to provide those sponsored some "surety" for their "financial and spiritual growth." And one more thing: the shared root in *sponsor* and *spontaneous* would seem to suggest that taking this kind of responsibility for another is "a natural, instinctive impulse."

The key to being a good sponsor is to follow through with your people, making sure they know what needs to be done in order to be successful.

## Following Through with New Distributors

You should have a check list for each of your new distributors. A sample of this kind of checklist is in the Appendix of this book.

This list will help you to remember what you have done and what remains to be done for each of your new distributors. It's your job to guide and support them in this business, especially during the early phases. Without your dedicated early assistance, very few of them will survive as distributors, and those who do make it will think of themselves as "Do It Yourself-ers." That's not a good way to run a Network Marketing business. Partnership is crucial for success in Network Marketing.

Some new distributors will be geographically located in such a way that many or all of your contacts with them will be by phone or mail. Others will be readily accessible to you, so you can drop by and see them in person.

## Helping Them Set Goals

Probably one of your first activities will be to help your distributors establish their business goals. Goal-setting is vitally important to goal-getting. As their sponsor, you should make the time to help your people establish their goals and decide what they want to accomplish in the business. It's very important to know what goals each of your new people have set. It will help you plan what you need to do to help your distributors achieve their goals. Write each goal down and determine steps to achieve them in your "Action Plan for Distributors." (You will find a copy of this in the Appendix.)

Once their business goals are established, your distributors can then determine what would be an appropriate inventory for them. Don't let them order inventory without establishing their business goals *first*. There is no need to frontload or overload on inventory. Most companies take a maximum of 10 days to two weeks to fill orders and will drop-ship products and supplies for their distributors. However, everyone should have all of the basic inventory and supplies on hand. When people are interested in buying something, when do they want it? *They want it now*. Distributors should have at least a two-week supply of products, kits, training materials and sales aids on hand at all times. Their goals will determine what is considered a realistic two-week supply. Your distributors don't need a lot, but there is an old saying, "You can't sell out of an empty wagon." That really applies here.

## Getting Them Started

After the introductory meeting is over, one of the first things you need to do is sit down with the new distributors and ask who they know that would be interested in the products. Work with them to create and prioritize their prospect list. Their interaction with you will help them add names to their list which they might have considered inappropriate before. Help them to develop the logic that goes with the emotion, so that when they wake up tomorrow morning, they not only have someplace to go and something to do – they will be going and doing with the greatest chance of success.

For example, their prospect check list may include a number of professional people. When they come to that section, they might be hesitant to consider these people as prospects, thinking they wouldn't be good candidates. If they say something to indicate this feeling, you should tell them that there are plenty of professional people who are happily involved in the company already. Give them their names, or explain how other distributors approached them. You can always provide encouragement by telling your new distributors how successful these professional people are in the company.

Your input is crucial. Otherwise, your new distributors will limit their vision of themselves and the very real possibilities of the opportunity.

After you have helped them develop their prospect list, give your new people a pep talk. Try to determine in which areas they may tend to sag. Maybe the new distributors are lacking in confidence or enthusiasm, or perhaps feel they don't have enough time to devote to the business. Don't try to cover too much at once or give the same talk to everyone. Just find out their immediate concerns, and encourage them in these particular areas.

## The Next Step – Training

Your next step is to invite them to an introductory training session. These sessions also serve as great booster shots. All successful, habit-changing programs involve regular contact with those who are going through the same life changes or processes. Some diet programs require checking in each day with a diet center, and other programs of a similar nature offer regular meetings where people can go for encouragement, a time of sharing and for mutual support. Your training programs offer this same kind of support. Not only will your new distributors receive great new ideas, but most of all, they will be reinforced by the positive attitude and "can do" approach of other distributors at the meeting.

Another area in which to offer your assistance is going over all the forms with your people. Paper work is a "necessary evil" in this business, and for some reason, many people find forms to be scary. People can feel very confident about their abilities and their knowledge of the product, and also about bringing someone else into the business, but forms can represent boring or intimidating work. Many people who are new in real estate say that they can find buyers and sell the homes, but they need help in filling out the purchase contracts during their first few months in the business.

It will help if you role-play some situations and actually have them fill out the forms to give them confidence. Confidence comes from competence, and nowhere is this more evident than in mastering what to do with the paperwork details of ordering and sponsoring. People have a tendency to get nervous when they fill out a form. Practicing several times before they actually do it with a customer or new distributor will help relax them and make them feel more in control during their completion phase in selling a product or sponsoring.

You also should offer assistance in helping them to understand the business. When someone is presented with a large number of new concepts, it is very difficult to grasp them all. There are so many at one time, it's hard to understand them all completely. We retain only a very small portion of what we see and hear, and it's only through repetition and continual exposure to the subject that we increase our powers of retention. Let them know that *there is no such thing* as a "dumb question." It's all right to ask *anything*. If they do ask something that you might consider simplistic or even stupid, don't let that feeling show on your face. Calmly and patiently answer the question and ask if they understood your answer. You should also provide them with additional reading materials for any area of the business in which they need assistance.

Remember, after years or even months, *you* possess a mountain of knowledge about the business. Most of us forget how long it took us to acquire all that knowledge. Have a little compassion for your new people and coach them through these initial phases of "information overload." It's always time very well spent, if for no other reason than when these people sponsor their first people, they'll do the same with them.

The next check point is to set up time for "tag along." This is a most effective training technique you can use with all your people. What it means is that they come along with you during your business day, whether you are delivering a product, making presentation calls, following up with another distributor or selling some products. They "tag along" to see what you are doing and eventually will become enthusiastic enough to say, "I want to do that, too. I can see how this will work for me?" Now, they really want to get going! Also, discuss with them everything you do. Tell them how and why, and do it by asking questions. "Did you notice how I used the money-back guarantee? How do you think that helped make the sale? How would you have done it differently?" One powerful benefit of this approach is that you're no longer dealing with a "raw recruit" – now you've got an *associate*! It takes over 1000 recruits to make a network – it takes only ten *associates* to make a prosperous Network Marketing business.

## Develop Their Management Program

Another key area in which they will appreciate your help is in developing their own management program. At first, this will be very basic, but as they mature and grow in the business, their management program will become more complex and powerful. Initially, you might need to introduce them to some time management techniques or systems. Many people don't even have a planning calendar or a daily appointment book. Other people have never used a "TO DO" list. Remember, a large percentage of good management is *self*-management. You don't need to be a management specialist in order to help people manage their time, their people and their lives. Share common sense principles that work for you. This is a great thing to do in a training session when you've got five or more people together. You'll get lots of fine ideas and the group will naturally support each other. The old saying goes, "He (or She) teaches best who teaches least." Let the group do the teaching for you. The ideas we champion best are the ones we thought of ourselves.

A small but often overlooked way to help is to take a personal interest in people's family lives. Often, people come into programs and business opportunities like this because it meets some of their "affiliation" needs. They need to be in contact with people they think really care about them and what's happening in their lives. Find out about your distributors' families – not all the intimate details, but whether they have a spouse and children and what they like to do. Inquire often as to their well-being. Keeping track of your distributors' families' birthdays, graduations and anniversaries. Sending a card or making a phone call will bring extraordinary returns. There's nothing you can say or do that will create a greater feeling of self-worth and caring for your distributors – *or for you.*

If your distributor shares an accomplishment, recognition or problem that another member of his family has, take note of it and follow through by making reference to it at an appropriate moment. If his or her son is playing on a championship athletic team at school, ask how they did in the play-offs. If they mention that someone in the family is ill or having a problem, when you make your next contact, ask if the situation has improved. Make whatever offer you're willing to make of help and assistance. Let them know you care about them as individuals, not just as business contacts.

Another important area you don't want to overlook is to assist your new distributors with their sponsoring sessions. It's a good idea for you to go with them on their first few appointments. Set it up in advance and tell them you will be contributing some ideas and comments, so they won't feel intimidated when you start to talk and think that you don't believe they are doing an adequate job.

Something you don't want to overlook is to introduce them to your own "upline" people. This can be very encouraging for them to meet the people who are responsible for your coming into the business, people who are as successful or even more successful than you are. Allow them an opportunity to share and pick up new ideas from these upline people. Remember, those above you have a vested interest in your distributors' successes.

What is the greatest fear shared by the majority of men and women in North America today – war, poverty, illness, death? No, it's the fear of the most dreaded disease in the world – *Public Speaking*. It's true! It's a very scary thing for many of your new people to set up and conduct their own introduction seminars. Work carefully and closely with them until they feel comfortable with what will happen there. Go over it verbally and on paper, and be there with them at their first few initial sessions. Help them evaluate the meeting afterwards, and give them constructive suggestions. Tell them about some of the mistakes you made during your first few sessions, so they will realize everyone is human and that an occasional "failure" in this area will actually help them to learn and grow to greater success in the business.

A friend of ours has what seems at first to be a rather ruthless but very effective approach for training people to conduct meetings. It's a two or three step process: first, he reviews with them privately a given aspect of the presentation – the company, the product, the plan…. Once he's sure they're on top of it, at the very next meeting, usually the third or fourth one they've ever attended, he calls them up to give that part of the meeting. Wow, are those people surprised! He never gives them a clue of what he's up to. They get up, knees knocking, and do that part of the meeting. Trial by fire! But he never calls on them until he knows they're ready, and he coaches them beforehand to make sure they know the material and can deliver it well. He also stands right up there next to them until he feels *they feel* secure – then he sits down. He's even been known to hold their hands through the entire section.

As if that weren't dramatic enough, he's got one other amazing twist. He co-presents meetings with new distributors the first three or four times they do them. Then, when he feels they're ready to go it alone, he helps them set up their next meeting. Fifteen minutes before the meeting is set to start, the phone rings. It's him: there's an emergency and he won't be able to make it. It's too late to cancel the meeting, so the new distributor takes a deep breath and does it himself. Again, trial by fire. All of this would seem foolish and insensitive if it weren't for our friend's remarkable ability to train people and give them his 100 percent commitment and support. He's a master, and his people are devoted to him and highly successful. It's become a kind of inside joke for the people in his Network, like an initiation rite, and they all know about it – *except* for the unsuspecting new distributor. And the audience always includes one or two of these seasoned veterans for added support.

## Help Your People Follow Through

It's important to help your new distributors conduct individual follow through sessions, too. Show them what you consider the fundamental elements of these sessions and let them sit in on some of your follow through sessions. Remind them of what you did and how you did it for them, and ask which things were most helpful. Once they go through this process, you can start to cut them loose and let them go out on their own.

After they have been in the business for a week or two, ask them if they have set up a business checking account. If they still have not set one up, make that an assignment they will complete before you meet with them again. If they seem reluctant, offer more assistance.

Encourage your new distributors in their self-development program. A number of times in this book we have touched on personal growth, and we can't overemphasize it. Personal growth will not only *go along* with the amount of money they earn – it will *lead* it. Make available tapes, books and self-improvement programs you use. If you don't have these programs available yourself, tell your new distributors where they can purchase or borrow these materials.

## Go for Three

Work with them until they bring in three new distributors. As a sponsor, if you will do that with each of your people, you will have done your duty and more. Your new distributors will then have the skills and the know-how to do it themselves.

As a sponsor, you should do each of these things for your new distributors and check off each duty on your list, so you won't overlook any items. Remember, there's a checklist for you to use in the back of this book. If you do these things for each of your people, you can be assured that they are getting the best possible training – which means they're off to a running start.

And this is just the beginning. Now, your job is to assist the new distributor with the other important details of organizing and successfully operating his or her business.

## *Chapter 12*
# What's the Best Structure for Your Business?

*This is a question that requires professional advice. Here's ours.*

# What's the Best Structure for Your Business?

## Proprietorship, Partnership and Corporation

Many Network Marketing distributors don't have a choice as to the form their business can take – i.e., proprietorship, partnership or corporation. Many companies prohibit distributorships from operating as a corporation. The basic reasoning behind these company decisions is that the relationship between the company and the distributor is a personal one, and the anonymity and the ability to transfer shareholders defeats that relationship. Some companies require one person with his or her individual social security number as the only name that the company will recognize as a distributor. Other companies permit distributorships to be corporations or partnerships, but may require disclosure of the principal parties involved and/or prior approval of the distributorship in writing from the company. Either form you select requires serious consideration. Choosing the best structure involves important business and tax planning decisions which *must be made* and which can affect your future dramatically.

Where incorporating is permitted by a Network Marketing company, many experts prefer the corporate form over sole proprietorship or partnership. Their primary reason is for the *limited liability* a corporation offers. That's because shareholders are limited in their individual liability with respect to the risks and responsibilities associated with conducting the business of the corporation.  However, this doesn't mean shareholders are totally without responsibility. They may be held personally liable if a corporation does not comply with certain recognized "corporate formalities." In order to protect shareholders from such personal liability, the corporation must operate as a separate legal entity, with corporate business matters kept separate from the personal finances of all the shareholders.

Entrepreneurs who operate as a sole proprietorship or in a partnership form, on the other hand, are "jointly and severally" liable (both as a group and as individuals) for claims arising out of the acts any one of them performed in the ordinary course of the business. An example of a potential liability problem would be if one of your customers had an accident or became ill and claimed it was a result of the product you – or one of your partners – sold them. Although your company would be responsible, because you are representing them, you may have to defend yourself against these charges as well. If you are a sole proprietor or in partnership, the case would be against you and / or you and your partners. If you are incorporated, the suit would be against the corporation, not against you personally.

The next reason for incorporation is taxes. Corporate tax rates traditionally have been lower than individual tax rates, and corporations historically have been given much more favorable treatment with respect to the deductibility of their contributions to retirement plans. The tax reasons for incorporating, however, have been substantially diminished after the Tax Reform Act of 1986. In many instances, individual tax rates may now be lower than corporate tax rates. And, sadly, the beneficial differences in how the deductibility of contributions to retirement plans have been treated have all but vanished.

One concern you may have about incorporating your business is the theory of so-called "double taxation." It could be a substantial drawback to your operation if you anticipate that significant amounts of income will remain in the corporation itself. Simply stated, if you make much more money than you spend paying your expenses and salaries, that "profit" is going to be taxed. When this excess income is distributed as dividends at the year's end, the shareholders have to pay taxes on those dividends. Since the corporation is a separate entity for tax purposes, it has already paid tax on this income once. When it distributes the profits (the "excess" income) in the form of dividends to its shareholders, they must pay taxes on that dividend income as well. Hence the term – "double taxation."

## C Corporation or Subchapter S Corporation – Which Is Best?

There is a method by which a small business owner may take advantage of the limited liability benefit of corporate status and still avoid "double taxation." You do this by electing that the corporation will be a "Subchapter S" corporation. Traditional corporations are classified as "C" corporations. Subchapter S corporations are those corporations in which *both income and losses* flow directly through to the individual shareholders. It's as if the corporate entity did not exist – for tax purposes. Now historically, the Subchapter S election has been used when you start a corporation that you expect will lose money in its early years. Those losses may be passed through and can be used as tax write-offs for those shareholders who have other sources of income against which these write-offs may take place. When individual tax rates were higher than corporate tax rates, no incentive existed to maintain Subchapter S status after the corporation started to generate income. Things may be different now.

Today, a number of leading tax experts are saying that in the aftermath of tax reform, Subchapter S corporations will blossom. They note that in many instances, individual tax rates will plummet well below corporate tax rates and it will be in the interest of shareholders to use the Subchapter S election. Whether or not you choose the Subchapter S election must be decided on a case-by-case basis with your tax advisor *after thoroughly evaluating* the comparative tax rates of the corporation and the individual shareholders. Your tax advisor should provide you with all the pertinent planning factors, such as intended accumulation of corporate profits or contributions to retirement programs.

Here's an example of what we're talking about:

Until your business has $50,000 of income, a C corporation has value because the first $50,000 of corporate taxable income is taxed at a lower rate.

As a tax saving tool, the possible use of the Subchapter S corporation definitely should not be overlooked. In all likelihood, you'll probably reach some balance between paying salaries to employees to take advantage of retirement and fringe benefit deductions, and the direct passage of income through the corporation to its shareholders, after making the Subchapter S election. In addition, you should consider the Subchapter S corporation for the purpose of transferring income to family shareholders who are in lower tax brackets. Since the income to share-holders who are children will be treated as individual income (and subject to parents' rates above certain thresholds), you can choose to make your children employees.

For a corporation to be treated as a Subchapter S corporation, an election must be made by the corporation within two-and-a-half months of the commencement of the tax year in which it will be treated as a Subchapter S corporation. The

S corporation will not pay tax, but will file a tax return on Form 1120S. Your income from the S corporation will be shown on your Form 1040 and, as with partnerships, you will receive a Schedule K-1 form reporting your income from the Subchapter S corporation.

## Tax Filing Requirements

There is an additional matter to pay attention to if you're going to operate as a sole proprietorship or partnership, as opposed to a corporation. In your full-time job, you may be accustomed to income tax withholding from your employer, but if you operate as a sole proprietorship or a partnership, *you* will be responsible for filing estimated tax payments at specific intervals through the year to cover your income tax and self-employment tax. If your self-employment income is $500 or more, *this means you*.

Network Marketing distributors, because they are independent contractors, will receive a Form 1099 statement of earnings at the close of the tax year from their Network Marketing company. No withholding will take place, because of your independent contractor status. You should be careful to reserve sufficient funds for your tax payments from ongoing earnings. If you don't, you may be in for a BIG surprise from the tax bill when the filing season arrives. In addition, if you pay commissions in excess of $600 to anyone in your downline, or sell consumer products for resale of $5,000 or more, you will have to file a Form 1099-Misc with the IRS, as well as provide the 1099 Form to those people in your Network Organization to whom you paid commissions.

If you operate as a sole proprietor, i.e., not incorporated or in a partnership, you will file Schedule C of Form 1040. If you operate in a partnership, you will file Form 1065. In addition, if your partner is not in your family, a separate Schedule K-1 will also be filed detailing the individual share of income, losses, etc.

Self-employment tax is the independent contractor's counterpart of the social security tax. Self employment tax is triggered at low earning levels and is reported on Schedule SE of Form 1040. Credit is given for income upon which an employee and employer has paid social security tax in other employment – i.e., if your Network Marketing business is part-time and you've got another job where you and your employer pay the SS tax.

Generally speaking, unless you have considerable experience in this area, it's best to seek professional help before you decide which type of business organization is best for you. Although we've touched on the major issues here, there are others. Corporations can have tax deductible expenses that individuals (sole proprietorships and partnerships) don't get. Some medical and dental coverage is an example. Also, there are some "intangible" benefits and liabilities for each different form of business structure. Personal and professional "standing" in the community, personal credit worthiness and the many implications of the success or failure of your business and how each may relate to your future, are all legitimate and very important concerns.

A bookkeeper is essential, but obviously not enough. A good accountant is also a must. But for decisions regarding business structure, we urge you to consider retaining an attorney with a strong background in business law. Although this may seem an excessive expense, especially at the beginning, your business counsel will prove his or her worth to you many times over in the course of building your business.

# Chapter 13
# Involving Your Family in Your Business

*For many people, Network Marketing is a family affair. The tax advantages alone make it worth considering.*

# Involving Your Family
# in Your Business

Because Network Marketing and direct selling businesses are often family affairs, the people who run these enterprises should be aware of the opportunities that exist for tax savings within the family business structure. With proper family financial planning, you can substantially lower your taxes. Two of the most important aspects of family financial planning are the tax consequences of hiring your children, and investments you make for them. The Tax Reform Act of 1986 made some changes in both these areas. A third tax saving strategy worthy of consideration is hiring your spouse.

## Hiring Your Children

Putting your children on the payroll can result in a substantial tax savings for the independent Network Marketing distributor. You can deduct their salary as a business expense and, since the child is employed by his or her parent, you're not responsible for withholding social security or federal unemployment tax on the child's wages.

The limitations of this arrangement are as follows:

1.   The salary must be reasonable in relation to the child's age and to the work performed. It must also be within the range of wages generally paid for that kind of work done in your local area. You probably couldn't pay your eight year old $20 per hour to stock shelves – unless that's what stock clerks make where you live. A good measure is to determine what you would pay someone else of the same age to do the very same work.

2.   The work performed must in fact be a necessary and required service to your business operations. Lawn mowing doesn't count, in most cases, unless you conduct interviews with prospective distributors or hold weekly meetings at your house – do you?

3.   The child must perform the actual work.

4.   You should document the hours and tasks the child performs, in case you are ever audited. This arrangement is what we call "aggressive" tax planning, and you should keep careful records for safety's sake. You might even consider drawing up contracts between you and your children, detailing the services they will provide and what they will be paid, in order to document the relationship. Contract disputes may be handled by your attorney, or by spanking or withholding TV privileges – or both.

5.   If you pay your children more than the exempt amount as discussed below, you may have to withhold federal income tax on their earnings and file the required forms.

6.   Actual payment must be made, preferably by a check from your business account for record keeping purposes.

Under the old tax laws, your child could earn up to $3300 without any tax liability, after taking into account the $2300 standard education deduction plus the $1000 personal deduction. But the new law has made some significant changes.

A child who can be claimed as a dependent on his parents' return can no longer rely on his or her own personal exemption. If you are claiming your child as a dependent, the untaxed income the child can make is limited to the amount of his standard deduction, which is $3000 in 1990 and thereafter is adjusted for inflation. This new law prevents the claiming of both a personal deduction by the child and a dependent deduction by the parent. But even if your child makes more than these limits and becomes liable for some taxes, you can still take advantage of the difference between your marginal tax rate and your child's lower rate.

Note that while the reduction in untaxed children's income effectively went from $3300 to $2450 for 1989, it went back up to $3000 for 1990 and further in 1991 because the standard deduction will be adjusted for inflation. This increase in the standard deduction amount will absorb some of the loss of the personal exemption. The net loss of unprotected income brought on by the Tax Reform Act of 1986 decreased to $300 in 1990, and probably will decrease further in following years.

Another setback imposed by the new tax law is the provisions for "unearned income" of children under age 14. While these provisions were designed to prevent parents from sheltering income by transferring income-generating property to their children, a side-effect is that if your child invests money he or she earns, the income from that investment that exceeds $1000 is taxed at *your* rate. If the child has substantial unearned income (from interest and dividends, such as being a shareholder in your Network Marketing corporation) in addition to what he or she makes as your employee, the computations are much more complex. When the child turns 14, all of the child's income is taxed at his or her own rate. The so-called "kiddie tax" on unearned income is not applicable to money your child earns as your employee.

The tax savings you can enjoy by hiring your children are apparent in the example of saving for your child's college education.

If you pay for your child's education from your own savings, you will have paid tax at your marginal rate on the money at the time you made it. If, however, you pay your child for work performed for your Network Marketing business, and your child puts the money in his or her savings account, then when the money is eventually used, you will have saved the *difference* between your marginal rate and your child's. If your marginal rate is 28 percent and your child pays no tax, then the difference you have saved on a college tuition bill of $5000 is $1400! That's a substantial boost to financing your children's education.

Since much direct sales or Network Marketing activity is conducted in and around the home, it probably is not difficult to find appropriate tasks for your children, such as taking inventory, delivering orders, answering the phone, secretarial work (such as typing letters), office cleaning, etc.

## Hiring Your Spouse

Sound tax and business reasons may also suggest that you should put your spouse on the payroll. Obviously, the spouse must perform appropriate duties and receive comparable salary to any other employee that would perform such a task. Although no tax benefits will accrue (as in hiring your children) by shifting income to a person in a lower tax bracket, at least two positive tax benefits will result. First, the employed spouse in a family business will not be subject to withholding of social security on his or her wages. A spouse's wages, however, are subject to federal unemployment tax. Thus, a shifting of income will take place that would have been subject to social security payments. Second, the transfer of income will create earned compensation for your spouse, thus allowing him or her to make tax sheltered contributions to an IRA or a qualified retirement plan, such as a Keogh or a profit sharing plan. This approach may be quite valuable, because you may have already reached the threshold limitation on contributions to an IRA or retirement plan. In this situation, however, you and your family may have succeeded in expanding the tax sheltering of family investments.

One of the oldest themes in the quest of taxpayers to lower their taxes is that of shifting income to a family member who's in a lower tax bracket. This method of tax planning is especially appropriate when you are planning for your children's education. Since the savings are really for the child's benefit, it seems fair that the savings should be taxed at their lower rate instead of your higher one. However, the Tax Reform Act of 1986 was a successful attempt to end many of the ways taxpayers had previously been shifting their income. Tax planners therefore must look harder to find the opportunities left over after tax reform. These opportunities do exist, even within the strict new framework.

Note: While our discussion focuses on *income tax* considerations, the investments and other arrangements discussed here will most likely have estate and gift tax consequences. You should discuss your individual options with your tax advisor.

*Income shifting* works because of the progressive tax table system, and because certain tax benefits are personal, such as personal exemptions, exclusions, and tax credits. Income shifting focuses on spreading out and using as many of these exemptions and exclusions as possible. The key to this strategy is the low-bracket taxpayer – typically minor children or elderly relatives who are your dependents.

The drafters of the Tax Reform Act of 1986 intended to close as many doors in the income shifting area as they could find. One door they found was that after a threshold of $1000, minor children are now required to pay their parents' tax rate on their investment earnings. In addition, children who are claimed as dependents on their parents' returns may no longer claim a personal exemption of their own. For children under age 14, the first $1000 in unearned income (interest, dividends or capital gains) is tax-free. Practically speaking, this means that a child can accumulate about $10,000 in savings before it starts to hurt. After that $1000 limit is reached, it's pointless to transfer more investments to the child. The income will be taxed at the parents' rate anyway. At age 14, income over $1000 is taxed at the child's own rate, presumably in the lowest bracket (15 percent). Therefore, income shifting once again becomes worthwhile once the child reaches 14. And again, before age 14, try to take advantage of transfers, if appropriate, as compensation or earned income with the child as your employee.

Clifford Trusts and Uniform Gift-to-Minors Accounts (UGMA) have been used by many parents as a tax-favored manner of planning for their children's education. Tax reform spells the end of the famous Clifford Trust, under which property was transferred to a child for a certain term, after which it reverted back to the parents. Income during the term was taxed at the child's rate. Now even children over 14 will be taxed at their parents' rate for income from Clifford Trusts or marital trusts set up after March 1, 1986. This also applies to new additions to trusts set up before that date.

Uniform Gifts-to-Minors Accounts will now be taxed as follows:

- The first $4000 of unearned income is not taxed.
- Additional money up to $500 is taxable at the child's rate.
- Unearned income over $1000 is taxed at the parents' rate.

After passage of the Tax Reform Act of 1986, some tax commentators reported that money given to children by their grandparents would not be taxed to the children. This is not so! The $1000 limit applies to *all unearned income* of the child's, including any interest on money the child has earned.

The requirement that children pay their parents' rate on investments can be avoided by switching children's investments to tax-exempt or tax-deferred securities, such as municipal or government savings bonds. The object is for the child to defer recognition of any gain from his or her investments until after he or she reaches age 14. At age 14, the investments can be redeployed, since the child's rate will govern the tax.

Some appropriate vehicles for tax deferral or exemption of children's unearned income are:

- Zero coupon municipal bonds
- Tax-exempt trust
- Municipal bond funds
- Single premium universal life insurance
- Tax-deferred U.S. savings bonds
- Growth stocks, as opposed to dividend stocks

Similar tax deferral or exemption vehicles should also be considered by parents for their own investments as well.

Your Network Marketing business may, for the first time in your working life, expose you to having more money than you thought was possible. With increased earnings comes increased responsibility. Again, we urge you to seek professional advice. Earning more money is great – keeping more of what you earn is even better!

# Chapter 14
# "Ask Not What Your Government Can Do for You..."

*How to make your partnership with Uncle Sam profitable for you, too!*

# "Ask Not What Your Government Can Do for You..."

## You and the IRS

**IMPORTANT NOTE:** These rates and regulations can and do change. Make sure to check with your accountant on any and every point. He or she will know the latest information that applies to you and your business.

One of the advantages of operating a home-based business is the ability to deduct business expenses from your gross income, just as in any other small business. For home-based Network Marketers, many normally non-deductible expenses may in fact be partially or completely deductible as legitimate expenses. If you meet the requirements for a home office deduction, substantial portions of the following expenses may become deductible:

*home repairs, property taxes, utilities and services (gas, water, electric, garbage, cleaning, etc.), insurance, telephone, rent, casualty losses, mortgage interest and depreciation.*

And, according to a recent ruling, you can even claim a partial deduction for purchasing, installing and maintaining a home security system.

Until 1981, the IRS took a very strict position with respect to claims by Network Marketing distributors for their home office deductions. It allowed a deduction only if the home office was used as the taxpayer's "principal place of business." Those Network Marketing distributors pursuing their business part-time were unable to take any deductions for their home office. Under this previous approach, the IRS maintained that an individual could only have one place of business, which was where the primary income was coming from. So, a full-time worker in a manufacturing plant could not take the home office deduction for his or her part-time Network Marketing business. The theory was that his or her principal place of business was elsewhere.

In recent years, happily, the IRS has liberalized its position. Under the current rules, the home office deduction is allowed as long as the home office is "the principal place of business for *any* trade or business of the taxpayer." (Emphasis ours.) Now, for example, a teacher whose principal place of business is her school, can claim a home office deduction for the portion of her home she regularly and exclusively uses to run her part-time Network Marketing business – as long as her home is the principal place of *that* business.

Congress trimmed back the deduction somewhat with the 1986 Tax Reform Act. Previously, the amount of the deduction was limited by the gross income of the business. Beginning in 1987, however, the deduction is limited by the *net income* of the business. So now you can only claim the deduction if your business makes money in the tax year, and you cannot deduct more for your home office than your business made. Congress' intent was to prevent home office deductions from being used to show business losses. However, the impact of this new limit is diminished by another new provision, which allows you to carry forward any home office costs that exceed your net income in any one year and deduct them in future years. Thus you can "save up" home office expenses you're unable to deduct right away.

The requirements for this deduction are very strict. You may take deductions for the business use of your home only if the business portion *is used exclusively and on a regular basis* as either:

1.  the principal place of business for your Network Marketing business – *or*
2.  a place where you meet or deal with customers or clients in the normal course of your Network Marketing business.

"Regular use" means that you use *a specific part* of your home for business on a continuing basis. Occasional or incidental business use of a portion of your home will not satisfy this requirement. "Exclusive use" means that you use a specific part of your home *solely* for business purposes – and for tax purposes, "solely" means 100 percent business use. Any personal use of the business space will result in loss of the deduction.

There is an exception to the exclusive use test: if you use part of your home, such as part of your basement or garage, for storing inventory. This exception is only available if all of the following criteria are met:

1.  The inventory must be kept for use in your Network Marketing business.
2.  Your home must be the only fixed location of your business.
3.  The storage space must be used on a regular basis.
4.  The space used must be separately identified and clearly suitable for storage – such as a basement, attic or garage, *not* a corner of the bedroom, kitchen, etc.

If your home office or storage space meets the tests described above, you must divide the expenses of operating your home between your business and personal uses. The amount of the deduction is determined by the percentage of your home you use for business and by the type of expenses you incur. You may calculate that percentage by dividing the number of square feet in your home office by the square feet in your house – or, if the rooms are approximately the same size, by dividing the number of business-use rooms by the total number of rooms in the house. A Network Marketing distributor who sets aside one room full-time in a ten-room house for his or her Network Marketing business activity may be able to claim one-tenth of all the housing expenses as legitimate business deductions.

Expenses are broken down into three groups. So-called "direct expenses" are those related to the specific area or room used for business and are fully deductible. Examples are painting, repairs, improvements, cleaning and casualty losses, as long as they apply only to the office and not to the rest of the house. In contrast, the so-called "indirect expenses" are those related to the upkeep and maintenance of the entire house and include all of the items listed above. These must be allocated to both business and personal uses based on the percentage of the total area of your home used exclusively for business. Non-deductible "unrelated expenses" are those that benefit only the non-business portion of your house.

In addition to the above requirements, you must keep records showing:

1. The part of your home that you use exclusively and regularly for business.
2. That you use this part of your home exclusively and regularly for business as either your principal place of business as a Direct Seller or Network Marketer, or as the place where you meet or deal with clients or customers in the normal course of your business.
3. The amount of depreciation and other expenses allocated to that portion of your home that is used for your business.

You can depreciate the portion of your home used exclusively for business, including furniture you move into it, but there is a catch if you sell your house. Ordinarily, when you sell your house and buy a more expensive one within two years, you may postpone recognizing any capital gain you make on the sale. However, you cannot postpone recognizing any gain on the portion you are using for business when you sell the house. Therefore, you should not claim the home office deduction in the year you sell or intend to sell your house.

If you have another job in addition to your Network Marketing business you run from your home office, your automobile expenses for driving from your home office to your other job may no longer be "non-deductible commuting expenses." Transportation between two business locations is a legitimate business expense.

For detailed information about this deduction, see IRS Publication 587, "Business Use of Your Home."

## Writing Off Your Home Computer

If you use or are considering the use of a computer in your Network Marketing business, you may be able to write off up to $10,000 of its cost. You must be able to prove that you use it more than 50 percent of the time for your business, but the smaller portion of its use can be for managing your investments, household budgeting, correspondence or whatever you want. You can also deduct the full cost of any software you purchase for use in your business (or for tax or investment purposes). If you have a home office, though, be careful where you keep your computer, or make sure it's easily moveable. If you use your computer in your home office for non-business work, you could lose the office deduction, because the office must be used exclusively for your business. Because the IRS is likely to view computer deductions critically, you should keep careful records of your computer use – when, how long, and for what purpose. There are software programs that run in the background as you use other programs that do nothing but keep track of the business and personal use. Their value is recognized by the IRS.

## IRS Audits – Try to Avoid Them

Tax audits are a very successful enterprise for the IRS. One leading business publication reports audits of 1983 tax returns produced $4.4 billion in taxes and penalties. The IRS collected an average of roughly $4000 for each audit it conducted. In the past, the IRS has audited about 1.3 percent of all returns per year, but the new tax law's crackdown on tax shelters may free more IRS personnel to scrutinize "unusual" or "questionable" deductions.

Network Marketing distributors should be rightfully concerned about being targeted for attention by the IRS. The principal reason is that much Network Marketing activity involves socialization and the use of personal assets such as homes and cars for business use. These types of deductions draw IRS scrutiny because for average taxpayers they tend to be personal and non-deductible expenses. The important question, then, is how you can decrease the chances that your return will be audited? You can take steps to reduce the likelihood that it will happen to you by being aware of how the IRS functions and of what "hot buttons" will make audits more likely.

The IRS doesn't reveal the procedures it follows when it selects returns for audits, but tax experts have developed a fairly accurate picture of what alerts the system from their own professional experience and from present and former IRS employees. The key to avoiding an audit lies in *being inconspicuous*.

The IRS begins with a scoring system for each return, in which items receive points related to their unusualness. The more out of the ordinary, the higher the score. This computerized system is called DIF – the "discriminate function system." DIF is intended to measure two things: the likelihood that you made an error or cheated on an item, and how much different your deductions are from everyone else's. If you score high enough, the computer flags your return for review by IRS personnel. If you have included explanations of any unusual items, those may bail you out at this point. It certainly won't hurt to have them. The exact scores required and the workings of DIF are closely guarded secrets of the IRS. The key to avoiding an audit is anticipating how this system will treat your return. Understandably, tax experts have carefully studied the results of this system, and can therefore make predictions which will help you stay out of trouble.

## Hot Buttons and Red Flags

Some of the factors concerning an audit obviously are beyond your control. The more money you make, for instance, the more likely you are to be audited. The IRS has also shown a statistical probability that those who are self-employed are more likely to misstate income and deductions than those on salary. You probably don't want to purposely make less or change your business in order to avoid an audit. But below are listed some IRS hot buttons on which you can have a positive effect.

The first category is one especially important to Network Marketing business people and Direct Sellers – business expenses. IRS tax examiners refer to deductions for home offices, business travel and entertainment (T & E) and business use of automobiles as "the kiss of death." Because they are often abused, IRS gives them closer-than-usual scrutiny and requires strict documentation. The IRS often challenges these deductions, knowing that many people do not keep the proper records and will not be able to defend their claims. Yes, it is a case of being guilty until you can prove yourself innocent. The obvious solution for the taxpayer claiming these deductions is to document carefully the expenses.

Several more generally applicable "hot buttons" are as follows:

• **Charitable contributions and casualty and theft losses.** Taxpayers who donate property to charities and taxpayers who have had property stolen or destroyed tend to over-value it for tax purposes. The best defense to an IRS challenge is to get an independent appraisal of the donated items.

• **Bad debts.** To claim a debt loss, you must show that the debt was a legal obligation, such as a contract or a loan note, and that you have tried to collect the debt. This is a suspicious deduction because many people try to claim debts of friends and relatives without satisfying the above requirements.

• **Hobby losses.** Any losses related to activities that appear to be more pleasure than business are sure to attract IRS attention.

• **Medical expenses.** Because the new tax law raised the threshold for deductions of medical expenses to 7.5 percent of adjusted gross income, the IRS is likely to be on the look-out for taxpayers who attempt to stretch medical deductions too far.

• **Extensive write-offs**, in particular, those from tax shelters. Even though the Tax Reform Act of 1986 cracks down on tax shelters, the IRS will still be watching. In the past, tax shelters have been the most consistent trigger of audits. Especially suspect after tax reform will be "tax-deferred" shelters.

• **Blacklisted Preparers.** Returns completed by preparers who have been blacklisted by the IRS.

• **Income from a barter-related activity.**

One leading business journal lists seven more factors on which revenue agents focus:

• **Comparative size.** An item that is much larger in proportion to the other deductions on the return will draw more scrutiny.

• **Absolute size.** A huge deduction, regardless of the accompanying deductions or the income shown on the return, will draw more scrutiny.

• **"Out of character" deductions.** If you claim a deduction that is very much out of the ordinary relative to the rest of the situation presented on your return, you are more likely to be audited. IRS materials give the example of a plumber with extensive deductions for airline tickets.

• **Mistakes, missing information, or incomplete forms** also draw attention. If it sees a mistake, the IRS is likely to suspect you of trying to mislead them. Make sure to fill in all the blanks the forms require, even if it's with a "0," a "no" or "not applicable."

• **Misfits.** Attempts to fit certain items into categories where they don't belong (in order to take advantage of more favorable provisions) will cause immediate suspicion.

• **Linked items.** If you claim one deduction but do not claim another closely related one, the IRS will wonder why. The same business journal gives the example that deductions for property tax and mortgage interest are usually found together (unless your mortgage is completely paid). If one is claimed but not the other, the IRS is likely to notice.

• **Comparative similarities.** If you claim more or larger deductions than other taxpayers in the general geographical area with similar incomes, you may become suspect.

It is easy to see why many of these "hot buttons" will arise for Network Marketing professionals. Because business people in our industry are home-oriented and social network-oriented, many of their deductions are legitimate expenses that average taxpayers simply wouldn't have.

The fact that these areas are targets is not to say that the deductions are not perfectly legitimate. As long as you can substantiate your deductions, you should not hesitate to claim them. What this target list does indicate, however, is that those companies and distributors involved in Network Marketing activity should carefully document and support their deductions, write-offs and business expenditures.

## Audit Avoidance Strategies

One way to head off a possible confrontation with the IRS is to include detailed explanations of any unusual items with your return. Even if the DIF system flags your return, an explanation may satisfy the IRS reviewer. The IRS does have some awareness of the characteristics of those taxpayers in the Network Marketing business. Its useful publication, "Tax Information for Direct Sellers" (IRS Publications 911), is available free from the IRS and describes many of the tax problems common in this business. It might improve your chances of avoiding an audit if you made sure that any explanation you include with your return clearly indicates precisely what your business is.

If you are considering an "aggressive" tax planning stance, you should also give thought to the relative value of claiming versus abandoning a given deduction. If you stand to gain a great deal and risk losing little, then an aggressive deduction is probably worthwhile. You should also think about the danger to your other deductions if an aggressive one triggers an audit. If a deduction is not worth very much, consider the merits of abandoning it.

Tax penalties are stiffer after tax reform. Congress is likely to approve of aggressive tax collection activity in the face of the huge national deficit. Penalties on cheaters are a politically benign source of money for the U.S. Treasury. Post-tax reform brings automatic negligence penalties of 5 percent of tax due and 50 percent of the interest. If you miscalculate to your own advantage by more than the greater of $5000 or 10 percent of the tax you paid, you will pay a 20 percent penalty!

If you are singled out for an audit by the IRS, you should contact your lawyer or tax advisor *immediately*. IRS "special agents" work for the criminal enforcement division, so if you are contacted by one, you should volunteer no information until you have consulted a lawyer or tax professional.

## Travel & Entertainment (T and E) Deductions

### • Business Meals and Entertainment

Tax deductions for travel and entertainment are especially important to those in Network Marketing, because of the importance of networking and personal contacts in this business. Business entertainment generally means the price of meals and drinks (including tax and tips), performances, sports events or anything with a specific business purpose. Unfortunately, the 1986 Tax Reform Act has reduced this deduction to 80 percent of the meal and entertainment expenditure, and the deduction must not be "lavish and extravagant." (The IRS decides what is "lavish and extravagant" under the circumstances on a case-by-case basis; there are, alas, no regulations for our guidance.) The cost of transportation to and from business meals such as cab fare to the restaurant, if otherwise deductible as business transportation, is not subject to this 80 percent rule.

"Passive" meals are out and "active" meals are in. The year 1986 brought the demise of the "quiet business meal."

Under the old law, it was enough if the meal took place in a setting that was simply conducive to business. Under the new law, you are entitled to deduct the cost of entertaining a customer, a "prospect," a distributor or other business associate, only if you can show that the entertainment is related to the active conduct of your business.

It makes a big difference whether you have a business meeting before or after the entertainment, or whether the entertainment is the only activity you attend with your business guest. The standards for entertainment that actually involve business are different from those where it merely accompanies your "doing business" too. The distinction is represented by the "directly related" and "associated with" tests.

If a meal directly precedes or follows a "substantial business discussion," then for the entertainment to be deductible, the discussion must be "associated with" the active conduct of your trade or business. This means that you engaged in a discussion, meeting, negotiation or other business transaction, in order to get income or some other specific business benefit, and that the business transaction was substantial in relation to the entertainment.

If no business discussion precedes or follows the meal or entertainment, then you must show it to be "directly related" to the active conduct of your trade or business. "Directly related" means:

1. You had more than a general expectation of gaining income or some other specific business benefit from the entertainment itself, i.e., your prospect was a good one.

2. You engaged in business discussions during the entertainment, i.e., whenever they blew the whistle, you got into the compensation plan.

3. The main purpose of the combined business and entertainment was the business transaction itself, i.e., bring the forms and applications with you; *and*...

4.  The expenditures were only for the taxpayer, his or her business guests and the spouse of any or all involved. To be able to claim a meal deduction, you (or your employer) must personally attend.

During 1987 and 1988, the full cost of a meal provided as part of a qualified banquet meeting was deductible. A "qualified meeting" included a meeting such as a convention, seminar or annual meeting if it met the following conditions:

1.  Expenses for food or beverages were not separately stated.
2.  More than 50 percent of those attending were away from home (that is, they qualified to deduct travel and over-night expenses).
3.  At least 40 people attended; *and*
4.  The meal was part of a program that included a speaker.

However, in 1989, the 80 percent limitation extended to these meal expenses as well.

Deductions for tickets to events such as plays, concerts and sporting events are now limited to the face value of the ticket, rather than the actual price paid. So, if you buy tickets through an agency or a "scalper" at the last minute at higher prices, you may still only deduct the face value of the ticket, subject to the 80 percent limitation. Some charitable sporting events are excepted from the 80 percent limitation.

## Entertaining Guests at Home

Network Marketing is a person-to-person business and entertaining business guests in your home is a commonplace, legitimate activity. You can claim a deduction of 80 percent of your out-of-pocket costs when you entertain at home. Remember, such entertainment must satisfy the "associated with" business test. The deduction covers food, drinks, catering, extra cleaning service costs, etc. If you invite both business and non-business guests, you may only deduct the percentage of the costs that corresponds to you and your business guests (and your respective spouses). Obviously, receipts are a must.

## Country Clubs

Entertaining your business guests at a country club is subject to further limitations, but if your use qualifies, you can deduct 80 percent of your club dues. You must use the club more than 50 percent for business purposes, and of that business use, only the portion that is "directly related" to your business is deductible – again, subject to the 80 percent limitation.

## Sky Boxes

Those scattered Network Marketing distributors who may own a share of sky boxes should be aware that Congress cut back the deductions many companies were taking for rental of sky boxes at sports events. The deduction is now limited to 80 percent of the cost of the same number of regular seats at the events as are in the sky box. Additional business entertainment expenses at the event, such as food and drinks, are (like regular business meals) 80 percent deductible.

## Travel and Meetings

Deductible travel expenses include air, rail and bus fares, automobile expenses, taxi fares, baggage charges for sample or display materials, meals and lodging while away from home, laundry and cleaning, telephone and other similar "on the road again" expenses. These expenses must be incurred for temporary living away from your regular place of employment.

Some key changes have been made in travel expense deductions. There is no longer a deduction for expenses of attending conventions and seminars unless they are for trade or business purposes. Under the new rules, you may no longer specifically deduct costs of attending personal investment seminars. Travel expenses for attending investment seminars may be deductible if they are closely related to the taxpayer's investment activities, but seminars at resort locations are likely to be viewed by the IRS primarily as personal trips. Seminars for which you may deduct expenses must offer "significant business-related activities," such as workshops, lectures, exhibits, etc. Travel expenses related to Network Marketing conventions and Network Marketing company training programs most often will meet this test. Deductions are no longer allowed for travel as a form of education, or for charitable travel expenses – unless there is no significant element of personal pleasure, recreation or vacation in the travel itself (which is hard to arrange for, much less stand). While you are traveling on business, your meals are 80 percent deductible, whether or not they qualify as business meals.

## Combining Business Trips and Vacations

You can save money on vacations *if* you plan them around business trips. In order for the business expenses, including transportation, to be deductible, you must show that the trip was primarily for business. But this does not prevent you from taking a few days for yourself as part of the trip. If you travel by automobile and take your family with you for the vacation portion, the entire transportation expense becomes deductible – *not* just your portion. Your spouse's travel expenses may be deductible if there is a legitimate business purpose in having him or her accompany you, such as helping you to establish personal contacts at a business convention. You should be prepared to show that this was the primary function of your spouse's travel. The more involved your spouse is with your regular business activities, the stronger this claimed deduction will be. Even if your spouse's travel expenses are not deductible, you can deduct the amount it would have cost you to go alone, even if you obtained a better rate for two people. So, if you take your spouse with you on a trip and spend $1000, and it would have cost you $700 alone, you deduct $700 rather than $500. If your travel is primarily for pleasure, then you may only deduct business expenses that are directly related to business activity. Also remember that traveling while looking for a job is a business expense. Again, the test is scheduled appointments, job interviews, etc.

## Luxury Water Travel

Travel involving an ocean liner, cruise ship or other forms of luxury water transportation will now be limited to twice the highest amount generally allowable per day of travel for employees of the executive branch of government, times the number of days in transit. There are special rules for cruise ship conventions.

## Foreign Travel Expense

Distributors often have good reasons to go abroad. Many Network Marketing companies operate in foreign countries, offering opportunities for sales as well as the sponsoring of foreign based distributors. Distributors also have reason to travel for meetings abroad.

If you travel entirely on Network Marketing business outside the United States, the travel expenses, including transportation, lodging, meals and entertainment, are deductible according to the same rules that apply to business travel in the United States. Under IRS rules, even if some personal vacation time is spent, the trip will still be considered entirely for business if you meet one of the following tests – which of course, must be carefully documented:

1. The trip was for a week or less (counting the return travel day but not the departure day); *or*
2. Less than 25 percent of the total time spent outside the United States was for non-business activities; *or*
3. You can establish that a personal vacation was not a major consideration.

If the trip is primarily for business but a personal vacation is associated with it (before, during or after), and you can't meet one of the above tests, then you must clearly allocate expenses between business and pleasure. Travel expenses to-and-from the business destination are figured by multiplying the total travel expenses by the number of non-business days, and dividing by the total number of days (counting both the departure and return days themselves).

If the trip, however, is primarily a personal vacation, you may deduct business-related expenses at the destination, but may not deduct the transportation cost. If the entire trip is vacation, then have a great time and forget the IRS!

The definition of what constitutes a "business day" can be very helpful to the taxpayer in applying for deductions. Travel days, including the day of departure and the day of return, will count as a business day. Any day in which the taxpayer is *required* to do business will count as a business day, even if only partially spent on business. A day in which business is canceled through no fault of the taxpayer will count as a business day. Finally, Saturdays, Sundays and holidays will count as business days even though no business is conducted *if* business is conducted on the Friday before, on the Monday after the weekend or on the days on either side of the holiday itself.

The above rules cover business travel by the distributor. Other more stringent rules exist for attendance at conventions and conferences outside the United States. However, with careful attention, distributors may maximize the tax deductions on such trips.

Inside the U.S., all travel expenses are deductible when the trip is primarily for business. The main difference when you are traveling abroad is that you must divide the travel expenses between business and vacation time. Travel abroad gets closer scrutiny from the IRS, so you should be especially careful about the rules for documentation. See IRS Publication 463 for further details, or consult your tax advisor.

The substantiation requirements for this deduction have always been strict, and they are even more stringent after the Tax Reform Act. The elements you must prove (and the records you must keep) with respect to your expenditures for meals and entertainment are:

1. Time;
2. Place;
3. Amount;
4. Names of those you entertained;
5. Business relationship, occupation or other information relating to the person(s) entertained; *and*
6. The business purpose for the entertainment, or the nature of business benefit derived or expected to be derived as a result of the entertainment.

For overnight business travel, you must record:

1. Time;
2. Place;
3. Amount; *and*
4. Reason for the expense.

Under the new rules, the taxpayer must substantiate each element of an expenditure with adequate records or by sufficient evidence corroborating the taxpayer's own statement. The taxpayer must maintain and produce such substantiation as will constitute proof of each expenditure. A contemporaneous log is not required, but a taxpayer must produce a record of the expenditure and business purpose made at or near the time of the expenditure, which is supported by sufficient documentary evidence. Documentary evidence has a high degree of credibility with the IRS. Receipts are required only for items costing $25 or more.

If a taxpayer negligently claims business meal deductions to which he or she is not entitled, a penalty of not less than 40 percent of the underpayment will be assessed. If the error is fraudulent, the penalty is 100 percent.

## Automobile Expense Deductions

Deduction of automobile expenses for travel remains substantially the same as before the Tax Reform Act. Automobile expenses must be incurred in connection with a business, trade or income-producing activity. For Network Marketing and Direct Sales people, business use of an automobile can include attending meetings, picking up or delivering both guests and merchandise, visiting your downline and upline people, trips to buy supplies for meetings or for your home office, trips to the bank for your business banking, and any other mileage you incur in the process of making or trying to make money. By combining business and personal trips, you can maximize the miles attributable to business and make your tax deduction bigger.

You can use one of two methods for deducting business automobile expenses. However, be careful which one you choose, because you can't change your mind – you have to pick one and stick with it. The first method is the *standard mileage deduction*. Under this system, you deduct 26¢ per mile for all business miles. The miles claimed under the standard mileage deduction must be substantiated, however the record keeping requirements are not as stringent as under the actual expense methods.

To use the standard mileage deduction, you must:

1. Not have claimed depreciation on the vehicle other than straight-line depreciation;
2. Not have claimed an additional first-year deduction on the car (the expensing deduction);
3. Not have claimed the deduction for more than one car at a time (but a husband and wife can each have a business car and claim the deduction for each car);
4. Not use the car for hire; and...
5. Keep a mileage diary that includes your business mileage, destination, the date and the business purpose of the trip.

After a vehicle has been fully depreciated based upon its use for business purposes, the standard mileage deduction is only worth 11¢ per mile.

The second method is the *actual expense method*. While it requires more record keeping, this method generally will yield a bigger deduction. This method takes into account all of the expenses of owning and operating a car and allows you to deduct the business portion. Included are expenses for gas, oil, maintenance (including such items as tires and batteries), repairs, insurance, depreciation, license fees, washing (even waxing and detailing) and interest on car payments. The record keeping requirements include all of those discussed above, and in addition, you must save receipts for all your auto related expenses.

The key to these deductions is keeping proper and complete records. *The IRS will only allow deductions that you can substantiate through your records.* While a daily log is no longer required, it is the most credible form of mileage records to the IRS, and it's still probably the best way to make sure you have complete records if you need them. If you use a credit card for any of these expenses, make sure to keep your monthly statements.

Other deductible automobile expenses:

1. If you lease a business car, your lease payments are deductible, limited by the business portion of the use. If you lease a car and use it less than 50 percent for business, the deduction is limited further.
2. Under both expense methods, you can deduct the business portion of interest on a car loan and any sales tax paid upon purchase of the car.
3. Parking fees and tolls on business trips are separately deductible (but not traffic tickets). Again, keep receipts and records of all your expenses.

## Commuting Expenses

If you have another job besides your Network Marketing business, and you have a home office that qualifies for the home office deduction, then the travel between your home office and your other job may no longer be non-deductible commuting, but *deductible travel between businesses.* However, the guidelines for this aggressive deduction are not entirely clear. Simply performing a few small tasks in your home office in the morning before leaving for your other job is probably not sufficient. If your home office qualifies for the deduction and you can show that you spend a substantial amount of time on your Network Marketing business *and* derive a substantial amount of income from it, you should have no conflict with the IRS over this deduction.

## Automobile Depreciation

You can depreciate the business portion of your car, just as any other piece of business equipment. For a car used more than 50 percent for business, you can deduct as follows: In the first year 20 percent, second year 32 percent, third year 19 percent, fourth year 12 percent, fifth year 11 percent and sixth year 6 percent.

If you use your car less than 50 percent for business, or if you calculate expenses under the standard mileage deduction, you can use only the straight-line depreciation method. Under this system, the percentages over the six year period are: 10 percent, 20 percent, 20 percent, 20 percent, 20 percent and 10 percent.

## Luxury Cars

Congress has limited the amount of the deduction you can claim for depreciating an automobile in order to prevent government subsidy of "luxury" automobiles. The rules limit deductions to $2560 for the first recovery year, $4100 for the second, $2450 for the third and $1475 for any other years cost is recovered. You can still completely depreciate a luxury car, but it will take longer than the normal five-year period. Thus the most expensive car you can depreciate within the standard schedule is one that cost $12,800.

## A Depreciation Tip for Two-Car Families

If you have two cars, one of which you use only for your business and one only for your family, you may be missing out on a substantial tax saving. This suggestion works, however, only if your business miles *exceed* your personal miles.

Case One: Suppose you buy two cars in 1990, each costing $10,000. You use one for your business and one for your family. You drive the business car 20,000 miles and the family car 16,000 miles. You can depreciate the business car, but not the family car. The depreciation deduction in one year is $2000.

Case Two: Same cars, same miles as in Case One, *except* that you drive each car 10,000 business miles and 8,000 family miles. Now, the business portions of both cars are depreciable, because both are used more than half for business. The depreciation you claim on each car is its price times the portion of business miles, times the first year deduction percentage, or $1600. Your total depreciation deduction for the tax year is $3200 – instead of $2000.

As a result of spreading out your use, you have gained an extra $1200 in deductions, effectively reducing the cost of the new cars. Note that in Case Two, since you are using the actual expense method for your business mileage (you can't depreciate and use the standard mileage deduction at the same time), you can deduct 80 percent of your upkeep and repairs for each car.

## Expensing

"Expensing" is an option of the taxpayer to deduct a large portion of the cost of an article immediately upon buying it, rather than gradually. The new tax law doubles the amount of this deduction to $10,000 for certain qualifying property. There are, however, several limits on expensing:

- The luxury car limits apply to expensing, so that the most you can expense in the first year is $2560.

- The amount you can expense is limited to the taxable income of your business. However, if you cannot cover the amount you wish to expense with your taxable income for this one year, you can carry the balance over into the following year.

- Expensing is only available for property used more than 50 percent for business.

## State and Local Sales Tax Requirements

Who is responsible for sales tax? When should it be collected? How should it be collected?

Dealing with taxes, of whatever form, ultimately must be faced by everyone. As the old saying goes, "You can't escape death or taxes." States and other taxing bodies will relent-lessly track their victims and take their toll, no matter how long it takes. As one philosopher put it, "The mills of the gods grind slowly, but they grind exceedingly fine" – and that applies to the tax mills, too!

Interestingly enough, the right of a state to collect tax on interstate sales, such as the kind of sales that occur frequently in Network Marketing, is impacted by the commerce clause of the United States Constitution, which prohibits states from unreasonably interfering with interstate commerce.

In one notable 1967 case, the U.S. Supreme Court held that a state cannot make an out-of-state seller collect a sales tax or use tax when the seller has only two contacts with the state in question:

1. If the seller only mails catalogs and fliers, *and*
2. If he or she uses the mail or common carrier to send customers the ordered goods.

The Supreme Court held that it was unconstitutional interference with interstate commerce to require mail order companies to collect a sales tax when those companies had no further contact in the state.

Network Marketing, however, has moved the art of marketing far beyond a simple interstate mail order business. Network Marketing does involve interstate sales of products, but it also involves one-on-one contact with customers and substantial activity within most states. Network Marketing distributors or sales representatives are basically independent, commissioned local sales people who (1) sell a product directly in the state, (2) procure sales orders for a company, (3) promote the product within the state, and (4) recruit other participants in the state to join the distributor's Network Marketing program.

While there are no specific cases which have decided that states may impose a sales tax on Network Marketing companies, it is generally conceded that states probably do have that right.

The question of the collection of sales taxes is further complicated in Network Marketing by the high percentage of personal consumption or use of company products by distributors themselves. Where there is personal consumption or use by distributors, no resale is made and no sales tax is collected from a retail consumer. It would probably not be difficult for a state to argue that for sales tax purposes, the actual retail sale in this kind of situation is the sale by the company to the distributor. In fact, some states specifically provide that independent distributors *must* pay a sales tax on a wholesale product which is purchased for their own personal use.

Network Marketing companies and distributors that do not treat sales taxes seriously may put themselves in line for some substantial penalties. Network Marketing companies usually follow one of three approaches to handling sales taxes:

1. Some companies collect the sales tax based on the suggested retail price at the time of the sale of the product to their distributors.

2. Some companies require distributors to get and to furnish the company with a state sales tax I.D. number, and to collect and remit the tax themselves for resale or personal use.

3. The third approach can best be described as "no action." In other words, the companies do not collect the sales taxes and remit them themselves, nor do they take any positive action to verify that distributors have obtained resale tax I.D. numbers and are following through on payment of sales taxes.

What all this amounts to, at least in the second and third approaches described above, is that *it is the responsibility of distributors* to become familiar with the sales tax structures and laws in their states and to comply with them. Granted, collecting these taxes and then paying them to the state is a real pain in the... wallet. It usually involves considerable paperwork and time that could be spent more constructively elsewhere in building your business. But taxes are here to stay. Treat them seriously. If you don't feel that you understand how the sales tax system operates in your state, hire the services of a good accounting firm. Let them set up a system for you to follow that will make the collection and payment process as painless and as accurate as possible.

However you decide to deal with your state sales taxes, by all means comply with your state's laws. It's just a reality of business life and will keep you out of a great deal of serious trouble. Make sure you know how your company handles sales tax responsibilities and that you do all that is required of you.

## Other Business Requirements

**Federal Requirements.** The federal bureaucracy has been quite active in restricting many of the commercial activities of our business. One agency in particular, the Federal Trade Commission (FTC) has been involved extensively in the regulation of Network Marketing companies and their independent distribtors. Your company should keep you informed of present and future laws regulating the industry, but there is one statute on the books that *every distributor or sales representative should know about*. It involves the basic structure of Network Marketing one-on-one contact, often in the home of the retail customer. These federal regulations are also often supplemented by various state laws.

Simply stated, these regulations grant a consumer the right to cancel a contract without penalty under certain specific conditions. The FTC rule, entitled "Cooling Off Period for Door-to-Door Sales," defines door-to-door sales as a sale, lease or rental of goods or services for personal, family or household use, having a purchase price of $25 or more, in which the seller personally solicits the sale and his buyer's agreement or offer to purchase is made at a place other than his main or permanent branch office. The rule requires that the door-to-door seller must disclose to the buyer the buyer's right to cancel the transaction at any time prior to the third business day (excluding Sundays and holidays) following the actual sales transaction. Disclosure is to be made by including a paragraph in the purchase agreement which reads as follows:

*"You, the buyer, may cancel this transaction at any time prior to midnight of the third business day after the date of this transaction. See the attached notice of cancellation form for an explanation of this right."*

Your company should provide this form and explain how to use it in the sales order forms they supply for you.

While the FTC rule is relatively simple, inconsistent state laws often make it difficult for the Network Marketing distributors to determine exactly what their responsibilities are in individual states. Once again, we urge you to check carefully with all government agencies about their particular requirements.

**State Requirements.** Since the early 1980s, more and more states have passed legislation aimed at Network Marketing distribution. These new laws often contain provisions for registration and disclosure requirements, cancellation rules, buy-back policies, participation standards and restrictions on earnings representations.

Various states require that registration reports be filed. These states require a wide variety of information in their registrations, including identification of participants, location of meeting sites, specific information about the principals of the business, explanation of compensation in the marketing program, explanation of buy-back policies, and explanation of investment requirements.

Most of these regulations are aimed at your company and its business relationship with you – rather than your relationship with your customers or the people in your Network Organization. However, it certainly would be to your advantage to be well acquainted with the laws regulating Network Marketing distribution in your state. Most of this kind of regulation is handled through the office of secretary of state, so check with that office first.

**Local Requirements.** Some towns and cities – and indeed, some counties – have passed statutes intended to regulate door-to-door, person-to-person sales. Check with your local authorities to see what regulations apply to you. Some municipalities have even passed laws regulating home-based businesses. These laws often prohibit signs, limit on-street parking in front of a dwelling on a regular basis, or provide a means of additional taxation. Often, people who have home-based businesses simply ignore these local regulations, but it would seem wise at least to find out what regulations are in effect, whether they have ever been enforced and what penalties are provided.

We know this is *a lot* of material. And we also know, for most of you, it's not what you got into Network Marketing to spend your time doing. However, we think three things are important for you to know here:

1.   These rules, responsibilities and regulations *are faced by everybody*. They are part of the context in which every single

business, regardless of size, structure, location, etc. must recognize, relate to and satisfy, in order to operate. What we're saying is: it's not personal – everybody has to deal with them; and, it's required – you *must* deal with them in order to remain in business.

2.    You do not need to master all these facts. You need to understand what they are and some of why they exist. All of this information is important for you to know about in order to make the kind of sound business decisions that will guide your enterprise into a profitable and lasting future.

3.    In the beginning, you will deal with these things directly. However, even in the beginning, make it part of your business plan to include professional expertise and assistance in these areas as soon as possible. There are men and women who love to learn about and work with the IRS and accounting and the law. That's their job. It's not yours. Render to Caesar that which belongs to him as soon as you can afford to – ie., get a very, very good accountant and an excellent lawyer you like and who likes you – and have them handle this for you.

Then you can concentrate on building the best, most successful Network Marketing business in the world.

*This tax advice is intended only for general information and resource purposes. It is neither legal nor accounting advice nor should it be regarded as a substitute for professional counsel on tax and business matters from your CPA, tax advisor, or attorney—a "must" for sound business planning. This book, however, should make discussions with your tax advisor more productive and efficient.*

# Conclusion

## Will *You* Succeed in Network Marketing?

Whether you are looking for the best way to join the entrepreneurial revolution or simply seeking a pleasurable and profitable part-time income – Network Marketing *is* your answer.

People from all walks of life are finding great success in this industry. Corporate executives, office and factory workers, housewives, students and professionals from every field of endeavor are participating in Network Marketing. There is no other possibility that we know of for beginning and building your own successful business which is so wide open and such a genuinely "equal Opportunity" for all.

Will *you* be successful? If you can simply and sincerely share your enthusiasm for a product or service with others... if you are willing to help them to do the same... if you are open to learning and passing on what you've learned... then *you will succeed* in your own Network Marketing Business. And "If" – as the famous poem by Rudyard Kipling says – is not so much a *question* as it is *the answer*.

> If you can keep you head when all about you
>> Are losing theirs and blaming it on you;
> If you can trust yourself when all men doubt you,
>> But make allowance for their doubting too:
> If you can wait and not be tired by waiting,
>> Or, being lied about, don't deal in lies,
> Or being hated don't give way to hating,
>> And yet don't look too good, nor talk too wise;

If you can dream – and not make dreams your master;
    If you can think – and not make thoughts your aim,
If you can meet with Triumph and Disaster
    And treat those two Imposters just the same:
If you can bear to hear the truth you've spoken
    Twisted by knaves to make a trap for fools,
Or watch the things you gave your life to, broken,
    And stoop and build 'em up with worn-out tools;

If you can make one heap of all your winnings
    And risk it on one turn of pitch-and-toss,
And lose, and start again at your beginnings,
    And never breathe a word about your loss:
If you can force your heart and nerve and sinew
    To serve your turn long after they are gone,
And so hold on when there is nothing in you
    Except the Will which says to them: "Hold on!"

If you can talk with crowds and keep your virtue,
    Or walk with Kings – nor lose the common touch,
If neither foes nor loving friends can hurt you,
    If all men count with you, but none too much:
If you can fill the unforgiving minute
    With sixty seconds' worth of distance run,
Yours is the Earth and everything that's in it,
    And – which is more – you'll be a Man, my son!

Yes, that is a tall order.  But the truth is that real and lasting success is not a result you accomplish at the end of the game "*If*" you score enough points. Success is a path along which you travel, learn and grow. What is so very special about Network Marketing, is that all of this success and more is actually available and achievable for you. Network Marketing is the path of success.

Given the right components – a solid well-managed company, a knowledgeable, supportive sponsor, a product or service that makes a difference in people's lives which *you* truly care about, and your willingness and commitment to help others be successful – Network Marketing is the *PERFECT* business opportunity! Powerful and profitable enough to attract the elite and already successful businessperson of today, yet simple and accessible enough to anyone to grasp as his or her own unique, personal path for a lifetime of financial independence, freedom and success.

Our very best wishes for *Your Success* –

Jeffrey Babener and David Stewart

# *Appendix*

A. Prospect List

B. Meeting Room Diagram

C. Checklist for New Distributors

D. Objective Worksheet

E. Action Plan for Distributors

F. Depreciation of Network
   Marketing Property

G. Reference and Resources

# Appendix A.
# Prospect List

Potential distributors are, literally, all around you. You'll find them among the people you know such as your friends and relatives. You'll also find potential distributors among your customers. Use the following categories to develop your initial prospect list. Remember, all of these people know others who may also be interested in your opportunity.

### AT WORK

People who don't like their job
People who are interested in new
 opportunities
People who are in a similar line
 of work

### IN NEIGHBORHOOD

College students who need extra
 money
Housewives with spare time
Landlord
Members of neighborhood watch
 club
Retired people who want to stay
 active

### PEOPLE WHO SERVICE ME

Bottled water reps
Diaper service delivery
Dry cleaners
Electrician/Meter reader
Exterminator
Firemen/Policemen
Gardener
Housekeeper
Mailman/Milkman

Plumber
Pool maintenance
Service station/Auto repair
Waiter/Waitress

### RELIGIOUS ORGANIZATIONS

Minister/Rabbi/Priest
Ministers of music
Religious education directors
Youth workers

### PROFESSIONAL
### RELATIONSHIPS

Accountants
Architects
Attorneys
Dentists/Orthodontists
Doctors/Chiropractors
Nurses
Optometrists/Ophthalmologists
Psychiatrists/Psychologists

### ATHLETIC OR SPORTS
### ORGANIZATIONS

Bowling club
Fitness center
Racquetball partners

Teammates
Tennis partners

## SCHOOL CONTACTS

Alumni association
Former association
Parents of children's friends
Teachers/PTA

## FORMER WORK CONTACTS

## SOCIAL CONTACTS

New and old acquaintances

## ORGANIZATIONS

Boy Scouts/Girl Scouts/
  Brownies
Lodges – Moose, Elks, etc.
YMCA/YWCA

## PEOPLE I PATRONIZE

Babysitter/Child care center
Bakery
Banker
Builder/Contractor
Carpet cleaner
Department stores
Druggist
Dry cleaners/Laundry
Florist
Furniture store
Furniture upholsterer
Gift Shops
Grocer and/or checkers
Hair stylist
Hardware store
Health spa

Insurance agent
Printer/Photographer
Real estate agent
Real estate appraiser
Rental stores
Shoe repair/Shoe stores
Tax service
Travel agent
TV repairman
Video club
Wallpaper store

## PEOPLE WHO TRY TO SELL ME PRODUCTS

All door-to-door or party plan
  salespeople like Mary Kay,
  Tupperware, etc.
Avon representative
Fuller Brush salesperson

## PEOPLE I HAVE BOUGHT THESE PRODUCTS FROM

Automobile salespeople
Carpet
Eyeglass or contact lenses
Heating fuel
Jewelry
Major appliances
Travel trailer
Water softeners

## RELATIVES

Family members, relatives and
in-laws as well as their friends

## NEWSPAPER WANT ADS

People who are looking for jobs

# Appendix B.
# Meeting Room Diagram

## Ideal Conditions

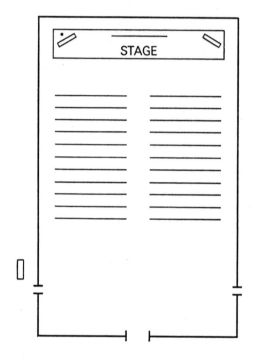

- 6" to 12" high stage
- Large chalk board and eraser; dustless chalk; lectern
- American flag
- Microphone with 30' cord
- Elevated product displays
- Theater-style seating, center aisle
- Entry door at rear of room
- Ceiling height at least 10'
- Lighting – fluorescent
- Floor – carpeting, no tile or wood

- No mirrors or windows
- Chairs – comfortable
- Colors – light rather than dark
- Registration table outside of meeting room
- Set up only 75 percent of the chairs and stack remainder in the back of the room
- Set room temperature 65° one hour early
- Set up water table in the back of the room

# Appendix C.
# Check List for New Distributors

**ACTION:**

- [ ] Read all company brochures, training materials and information provided
- [ ] List any questions you need answered
- [ ] Become familiar with all products
- [ ] Fill out Objective Worksheet
- [ ] Fill out Action Plan
- [ ] Order product
- [ ] Make a list of prospects
- [ ] Study company manual
- [ ] Open a business checking account
- [ ] Order rubber stamp with name, address, phone number
- [ ] Decide on a business name
- [ ] File a business name if you elect to use one
- [ ] Acquire a sales tax license if needed
- [ ] Organize an office area
- [ ] Set up files for prospects, sales, distributors, tax information, etc.
- [ ] If possible set up a product display area
- [ ] Study marketing plan
- [ ] Order sales aids and literature from company
- [ ] Invest in a tape recorder if you don't have one
- [ ] Borrow or invest in self-improving tapes and books
- [ ] Spend some time each day improving your mind and attitude
- [ ] Attend an introductory seminar and take a guest with you
- [ ] Sponsor your first distributor

# Appendix D.
# Objective Worksheet

1.  What is your first year objective as a distributor?


2.  How many people are you going to need in your organization?


3.  How much time do you feel it will require each week?


4.  What strengths do you have that will assist you in reaching this objective?


5.  What weaknesses or problem areas might tend to hold you back?


6.  Is your objective realistic?


7.  How would you feel if you didn't reach it?


8.  Vividly imagine yourself reaching your objective. How does it feel?


9.  Are you going to need the cooperation of "significant others" in your life? If so, what steps can you take to ensure their assistance?


10. What will you need to invest in sales aids and inventory to do business?

# Appendix E.
# Action Plan for Distributors

In order to achieve the objectives I have stated and obtain the things I want out of my life, I am going to commit myself to the following goals.

## EACH DAY I WILL:

Contact _____ people about our products

Contact _____ people about becoming a distributor

## EACH WEEK I WILL:

Attend _____ meetings

Contact _____ downline people

Use company products _____ times

Retail _____ of products

Recruit _____ new distributors

Follow up on _____ distributors

## EACH MONTH I WILL:

Bring _____ people to an Introductory Seminar

Conduct _____ Introductory Seminars

Attend _____ training sessions

## THIS YEAR I WILL:

Conduct _____ training sessions

Develop _____ leaders

# Appendix F.
# Depreciation of
# 'Network Marketing Property'

Because Network Marketing business people so often use their own homes and automobiles for business purposes, they can depreciate these assets (though frequently they don't realize it) just as any other business depreciates its equipment. Depreciation is an effective way to obtain tax relief on items used for a home business or for combined personal and business use. Some of the articles you can depreciate are: typewriters, copiers, computers, calculators, automobiles (new or used), office furniture, tape recorders, VCRs, projectors, other business machines and your home office itself.

Knowing the mechanics of capital expenditures and depreciation can save individuals who own home-based businesses major tax dollars and these savings make it possible to buy needed business equipment. This section is an initial explanation of the depreciation of some business property used by many Network Marketing and Direct Sales people. The discussion here is particularly applicable to depreciation of property you put into service on or after January 1, 1987. Consult your tax advisor for information relating to depreciation for equipment you placed in service in previous years.

Depreciation, or "capital cost recovery," is the means by which you recover the capital you have invested in property you use in business, trade or income-seeking activity. The rationale behind the deduction is to allow for the exhaustion, wear and tear on the property, and to spread the cost over its useful life span. Depreciation works differently for different types of property.

Property is depreciable if it meets these requirements:

1.  It must be used in business or held for the production of income.

2.  It must have a determinable life that must be longer than one year.

3.  It must be something that wears out, decays, gets used up, becomes obsolete or loses value from natural causes.

In general, if property does not meet all three of these conditions, it is not depreciable. Depreciable property is also called "recoverable property."

If you use a piece of property for both business and personal use, you may deduct depreciation only for the business portion. For certain kinds of property, however, there are special limits on the deduction if the business portion of your use is less than 50 percent, *and* you placed the equipment in service after June 18, 1987. This property is referred to as "listed property," and it includes passenger automobiles, home computers and any property of a type generally used for entertainment, recreation or amusement, including photographic, phonographic, communication and video recording equipment. You cannot expense listed property, and you can depreciate this property only on the straight-line method over the prescribed class life. Congress added these limits because it found that taxpayers were often claiming business deductions for items that were actually personal. While these items often are used by Network Marketing people for legitimate business purposes, the stricter tax regulations still apply.

The 1986 Tax Reform Act included an overhaul of the entire depreciation system. In general, deductions for depreciation will be smaller each year, because the statutory lives of equipment have been extended, and because the lower tax rates reduce the value of those deductions. However, the new tax law provides for bigger deductions in the first two years after initial purchase. Thus, you can recover more value in a shorter period, even if the useful life of the equipment is considered to be longer.

You figure depreciation deductions for recovery property under ACRS, the "Accelerated Cost Recovery System." (Since the 1986 modifications, the system is sometimes referred to as MACRS – "Modified Accelerated Cost Recovery System.") ACRS was designed to introduce some uniformity into the write-off periods for similar kinds of property. It applies to both new and used recovery property. The way ACRS applies depends on what kind of property it is and when you placed it into service. You may also choose to use a longer cost-recovery system, the straight-line depreciation method, under which you deduct the same amount of depreciation each year.

Congress has established arbitrary class lives for certain kinds of property, and theses lives have changed with tax reform. Automobiles and computers are now five-year properties; office equipment is seven-year property. For personal property placed in service after 1986, depreciation generally is figured on the "200 percent declining balance method," which means that the first year deductions are twice those applied under the straight-line depreciation method. This approach, termed the "half-year convention," effectively cuts the first year's deduction in half. Only half of the deduction is allowed in the year the asset is bought. Therefore, the cost of the five-year property is actually recovered over six years, because only half of the allowance is recoverable in the first year. The balance of the first year allowance is recovered in the sixth year. Thus the actual recovery period is one year longer than the "class" label of the property. A further limitation applies if more than 40 percent of the equipment you buy in a year is placed in service in the last quarter, in which case the first-year deduction shrinks even further.

## Putting Used Equipment into Service

You may wish to "press into service" items that have until now been personal, such as a car, home computer or VCR. Perhaps you are moving a couch or a typewriter into your home office. When you convert personal property to business use, the basis you use for depreciation is the lesser of:

1. The fair market value of the property at the date of the change; or

2. Your original cost or other basis of the property, plus the cost of improvements and minus any previously claimed casualty loss deductions.

"Fair market value" is the price at which the property would change hands between a buyer and a seller, neither being *required* to buy or sell, and both having reasonable knowledge of all the necessary facts. Sales of similar property on or about the same date may be helpful in figuring fair market value.

## Disposal of Depreciated Property

When personal property that has been depreciated is sold, the gain is "recaptured" and treated as ordinary income to the extent of the total depreciation deductions previously claimed on it. When you dispose of property before its statutory class life has expired, you cannot claim a depreciation deduction for that year.

## Investment Tax Credit

One setback for business after tax reform is the repeal of the investment tax credit. This allowed businesses to take credits against their taxes of up to 10 percent of the cost of tangible depreciable property, such as office equipment and automobiles. The new law abolishes this, retroactive to January 1, 1986. The new law also reduces any credits carried over from previous years by 35 percent.

## Expensing

"Expensing" is an option of the taxpayer to deduct a large portion of the cost of an article immediately upon buying it, rather than gradually. Expensing is one area where the new tax law is especially favorable to small businesses. Under the old law, a taxpayer could elect to deduct, as an immediate expense deduction, up to $5000 or the cost of newly acquired depreciable personal property. The new tax law doubles this to $10,000 for certain qualifying property. The amount you can write off for expensing, however, is limited to the taxable income of your business. If you cannot cover the amount you wish to expense with your taxable income for the year, you can carry over the balance into the following year.

Congress has limited the benefits of this write-off to small businesses by providing that after $200,000 worth of business equipment is placed in service during the year, the $10,000 expensing limit is reduced dollar for dollar by additional expenditures, wiping out the deduction when $210,000 in equipment costs is reached.

A caveat on expensing is that it is only available for property used more than 50 percent for business, and of course, you cannot depreciate the part of an equipment purchase that you expense.

Specific schedules for allowable expense deductions change from year to year; for guidelines, consult a tax professional, accountant or financial advisor.

# Appendix G.
# References and Resources

## Training Literature

*The Network Marketer's Guide to Success*, By Jeffrey A. Babener and David Stewart © 1990: a book on how to build a successful network marketing business, available in quantity discounts; Success In Action, P.O. Box 5918, Scottsdale AZ 85261, tel. 602-951-4551 / 949-5761.

*Network Marketing: One Plus One Equals Four*, By Jeffrey A. Babener and David Stewart © 1990: an introductory brochure, available in bulk discounts; Success In Action, P.O. Box 5918, Scottsdale AZ 85261, tel. 602-951-4551 / 949-5761.

*Network Marketing: One Plus One Equals Four*, cassette, by Jeffrey A. Babener and David Stewart © 1990: an introductory brochure on audio cassette, available in bulk discounts, Success In Action, P.O. Box 5918, Scottsdale AZ 85261, tel. 602-951-4551 / 949-5761.

*Building A Successful Network Marketing Business*, by David Stewart; a 4-cassette audio album plus 36-page workbook; Success In Action, P.O. Box 5918, Scottsdale AZ 85261, tel. 602-951-4551 / 949-5761.

*Tax Guide For MLM / Direct Selling Distributors*, By Jeffrey A. Babener, J.D., © 1987: Legal Line® Publications, 101 S.W. Main St., Suite 600, Portland, Oregon 97204, tel. 503-226-6600.

# About the Authors

JEFFREY BABENER is a prolific author, speaker and lecturer, and is widely acknowledged as the "premiere attorney for Network Marketing in the United States" – which means the world.  He is the author of the best-selling MLM business text, *Tax Guide For MLM/Direct Selling Distributors*.   He serves on the Lawyer's Council for the Direct Selling Association and is General Counsel for the Multi-Level Marketing International Association – the two professional trade organizations for the Network Marketing industry.  He is a graduate of the University of Southern California Law School where he was an editor of the *Law Review*. An active member of the California and Oregon bars, his law firm (Babener & Orcutt, 101 S.W. Main St., Suite 600, Portland, Oregon 97204) serves leading Network Marketing companies with annual sales in excess of $2 billion.

On the personal side, Jeff Babener is a soft-spoken man whose youthful appearance and affable manner seem in quiet opposition to his demanding professional responsibilities and schedule.  On any given day, a call to his office will be returned by him from Dallas, Washington, Chicago, Australia, Canada, Great Britain or from any of two-dozen airports or from a plane 40,000 feet in the air.

Jeffrey lives in Portland with his wife, Roz, who teaches school, his son Jeremy and his daughters Rebecca and Rachel.  The Babeners are an avid outdoor family who enjoy hiking, camping, backpacking, fishing, white-water rafting, and just about every endeavor that involves the outdoors.

How does Jeff make the time for all of this?  As he says, "If you truly love what you are doing – you can always find the time."

DAVID STEWART is a leader of leaders. He is a trainer, consultant, sales motivator and educator. In his more than 20 years in Network Marketing, he has successfully served in every position from Distributor to Director of Training, from Sales Manager to Board of Directors of the Multi-Level Marketing International Association and is the president and founder of the widely acclaimed field sales leadership firm, Success In Action (PO Box 5918, Scottsdale, Arizona 85261). David has worked with a vast number of Network Marketing's leading corporations, including Sunrider, Matol Botanical International, Network 2000, Shaklee Corporation and hundreds of others. Along with Jeffrey Babener, David has authored the tremendously successful booklet *One Plus One Equals Four*, used throughout North America by thousands of distributors as a positive professional presentation of the benefits of a Network Marketing career.

David lives with his wife, Linda, and four teenagers, Dana, Julie, James and Dan, in Scottsdale. His passion is gardening. As he says, "I'm either in a business suit – or in a pair of frayed jeans digging, planting and taking care of the land."

David's approach to his personal and professional life is the same. "By serving a common purpose that is larger than we are, and working together with and for each other, we'll become stronger and more inspired individuals. In the process, we'll each accomplish our life's goals and fulfill our true destiny."

# Index